THE WORD

FOR YOUR EVERY NEED

Harrison House

Tulsa, Oklahoma

Revised Printing 2013

The Word for Your Every Need
ISBN 978-160683-749-8
Copyright © 1993 by Harrison House
P. O. Box 35035
Tulsa, Oklahoma74153

Presented to

_____

By

_____

Date

_____

Occasion

_____

THE INSPIRED WORD

OF GOD

Nautical charts are used by sailors and maps are used by road travelers as their guidebooks and keys to their final destinations. Christians have a map and guidebook that is far superior to any other in the world —the Bible. This book is not just a great piece of literature; it is the main ingredient to a successful Christian life. The Bible should be read daily, consulted constantly and studied carefully. The Scriptures are the inspired Word of God. Second Timothy 3:16,17 says:

All scripture is given by inspiration of God, and is profitable for doctrine, for reproof, for correction, for instruction in righteousness: That the man of God may be perfect, thoroughly furnished unto all good works.

It is obvious from this passage that the Lord gave us His Word for specific reasons: to confirm our beliefs, to set spiritual and moral guidelines, to give us godly inspiration and wisdom for our daily living, and to instruct us in the ways of our Father. We cannot draw these things from the Word of God without daily study.

CONTENTS

Priorities in Your Life

The Priority of Knowing Jesus
As Your Savior   1
The Priority of Being Filled With the Holy Spirit   5
The Priority of Hungering and
Seeking for God With All Your Heart   9
The Priority of Obedience to God   14
The Priority of God's Word   16
The Priority of Prayer   18
The Priority of Praise and Worship   21
The Priority of Attending Your Local Church   24
The Priority of Witnessing and Spreading the Gospel   26

When You Want To Be...

When You Want To Be Patient   32
When You Want To Be Loving   35
When You Want To Be Giving   39
When You Want To Be Godly   42
When You Want To Be Diligent   46
When You Want To Be Honest   48
When You Want To Be Understanding   51
When You Want To Be Joyful   55
When You Want To Be Courageous   57

When You Want To Be Compassionate   60
When You Want To Be Consistent   62
When You Want To Be a Leader   64
When You Want To Be Faithful   67
When You Want To Be Considerate   70

When You Need...

When You Need To Pray   73
When You Need Forgiveness   77
When You Need To Forgive   80
When You Need Faith   83
When You Need Comfort   86
When You Need Encouragement   90
When You Need Joy   94
When You Need Healing   97
When You Need Love   101
When You Need Patience   106
When You Need Peace   110
When You Need Protection   114
When You Need Self-Control   116
When You Need Strength   120
When You Need Wisdom   122
When You Need Deliverance   126
When You Need Inner Peace   129
When You Need Discernment   133
When You Need Ability   134

When You Need a Friend 137

When You Need Motivation 138

When You Need Favor 141

When You Need To Apologize 143

When You Need To Overcome Anger 145

When You Need To Overcome Resentment 148

When You Need To Overcome Envy Jealousy 149

When You Need Finances 151

When You Need Guidance 155

When You Are...

When You Are Anxious 160

When You Are Angry 163

When You Are Confused 165

When You Are Disappointed 169

When You Are Frustrated 171

When You Are Insecure 174

When You Are Jealous 177

When You Are Lonely 179

When You Are Persecuted 181

When You Are Uncertain 185

When You Are Choosing a Career 186

When You Are Afraid of the Future 188

When You Are Looking for a Job 189

When You Are Facing Marital Problems 191

When You Are Overworked 194

When You Are Under Stress   196

When You Are Offended   201

When You Are Unfulfilled   203

When You Feel...

When You Feel Disorganized   205

When You Feel Overwhelmed   207

When You Feel Robbed of Your Private Time   209

When You Feel Unqualified for Leadership   211

When You Feel Resentful   213

When You Feel Like a Failure   216

When You Feel Threatened   218

When You Feel Betrayed   221

When You Feel Used   226

When You Feel Like Compromising   229

When You Feel Like Giving Up   231

When You Feel Incapable of Achieving
Your Goals and Dreams   235

When You Feel Anxious About Getting Older   237

When You Feel Unfulfilled   238

*As the rain and the
snow come down
from heaven,
and do not return to it
without watering the earth
and making it bud and flourish,
so that it yields seed
for the sower
and bread for the eater,
so is my word that goes out from
my mouth:
It will not return
to me empty,
but will accomplish what
I desire and achieve the
purpose for which
I sent it.*

Isaiah 55:10,11

Priorities in Your Life

The Priority of Knowing
Jesus As Your Savior

Just as Moses lifted up the snake in the desert, so the Son of Man must be lifted up, That everyone who believes in him may have eternal life.

For God so loved the world that he gave his one and only Son, that whoever believes in him shall not perish but have eternal life.

For God did not send his Son into the world to condemn the world, but to save the world through him.

Whoever believes in him is not condemned, but whoever does not believe stands condemned already because he has not believed in the name of God's one and only Son.

John 3:14-18

In reply Jesus declared, "I tell you the truth, no one can see the kingdom of God unless he is born again."

John 3:3

For my Father's will is that everyone who looks to the Son and believes in him shall have eternal life, and I will raise him up at the last day.

John 6:40

The Father loves the Son and has placed everything in his hands. Whoever believes in the Son has eternal life, but whoever rejects the Son will not see life, for God's wrath remains on him.

John 3:35, 36

For just as the Father raises the dead and gives them life, even so the Son gives life to whomhe is pleased to give it.

Moreover, the Father judges no one, but has entrusted all judgment to the Son, That all may honor the Son just as they honor the Father. He who does not honor the Son does not honor the Father, who sent him.

I tell you the truth, whoever hears my word and believes him who sent me has eternal life and will not be condemned; he has crossed over from death to life.

I tell you the truth, a time is coming and has now come when the dead will hear the voice of the Son of God and those who hear will live.

For as the Father has life in himself, so he has granted the Son to have life in himself.

And he has given him authority to judge because he is the Son ofMan.

John 5:21-27

I tell you the truth, he who believes has everlasting life. I am the bread of life.

John 6:47,48

But he continued, "You are from below; I am from above. You are of this world; I am not of this world.

"I told you that you would die in your sins; if you do not believe that I am [the one I claim to be], you will indeed die in your sins."

John 8:23,24

The Priority of Knowing Jesus As Your Savior

The thief comes only to steal and kill and destroy; I have come that they may have life, and have it to the full.

John 10:10

My sheep listen to my voice; I know them, and they follow me.

I give them eternal life, and they shall never perish; no one can snatch them out of my hand.

My Father, who has given them to me, is greater than all; no one can snatch them out of my Father's hand.

I and the Father are one.

John 10:27-30

Jesus said to her, "I am the resurrection and the life. He who believes in me will live, even though he dies;

"And whoever lives and believes in me will never die. Do you believe this?"

John 11:25,26

For there is one God and one mediator between God and men, the man Christ Jesus,

Who gave himself as a ransom for all men—the testimony given in its proper time.

1 Timothy 2:5,6

Then Jesus cried out, "When a man believes in me, he does not believe in me only, but in the one who sent me.

"When he looks at me, he sees the one who sent me.

I have come into the world as a light, so that no one who believes in me should stay in darkness."

John 12:44-46

Jesus answered, "I am the way and the truth and the life. No one comes to the Father except through me."

John 14:6

And everyone who calls on the name of the Lord will be saved.

Acts 2:21

Peter replied, "Repent and be baptized, every one of you, in the name of Jesus Christ for the forgiveness of your sins. And you will receive the gift of the Holy Spirit."

Acts 2:38

Repent, then, and turn to God, so that your sins may be wiped out, that times of refreshing may come from the Lord.

Acts 3:19

Then know this, you and all the people of Israel: It is by the name of Jesus Christ of Nazareth, whom you crucified but whom God raised from the dead, that this man stands before you healed.

He is "the stone you builders rejected, which has become the capstone."

Salvation is found in no one else, for there is no other name under heaven given to men by which we must be saved.

Acts 4:10-12

No! We believe it is through the grace of our Lord Jesus that we are saved, just as they are.

Acts 15:11

For it is by grace you have been saved, through faith — and this not from yourselves, it is the gift of God—

Not by works, so that no one can boast.

Ephesians 2:8,9

The Priority of Being Filled With the Holy Spirit

If you then, though you are evil, know how to give good gifts to your children, how much more will your Father in heaven give the Holy Spirit to those who ask him!

Luke 11:13 And with that he breathed on them and said, "Receive the Holy Spirit."

John 20:22

Do not get drunk on wine, which leads to debauchery. Instead, be filled with the Spirit.

Ephesians 5:18

All of them were filled with the Holy Spirit and began to speak in other tongues as the Spirit enabled them.

Acts 2:4

When the apostles in Jerusalem heard that Samaria had accepted the word of God, they sent Peter and John to them.

When they arrived, they prayed for them that they might receive the Holy Spirit.

Because the Holy Spirit had not yet come upon any of them; they had simply been baptized into the name of the Lord Jesus.

Then Peter and John placed their hands on them, and they received the Holy Spirit.

Acts 8:14-17

Then Ananias went to the house and entered it. Placing his hands on Saul, he said, "Brother Saul, the Lord —Jesus, who appeared to you on the road as you were coming here —has sent me so that you may see again and be filled with the Holy Spirit."

Acts 9:17

While Peter was still speaking these words, the Holy Spirit came on all who heard the message.

The circumcised believers who had come with Peter were astonished that the gift of the Holy Spirit had been poured out even on the Gentiles.

For they heard them speaking in tongues and praising God. Then Peter said,

"Can anyone keep these people from being baptized with water? They have received the Holy Spirit just as we have"

Acts 10:44-47

God, who knows the heart, showed that he accepted them by giving the Holy Spirit to them,just as,he did to us.

He made no distinction between us and them, for he purified their hearts by faith.

Acts 15:8, 9

And asked them, "Did you receive the Holy Spirit when you believed?" They answered, "No, we have not even heard that there is a Holy Spirit."

So Paul asked, "Then what baptism did you receive?" "John's baptism," they replied.

Paul said, "John's baptism was a baptism of repentance. He told the people to believe in the one coming after him, that is, in Jesus."

On hearing this, they were baptized into the name of the Lord Jesus.

When Paul placed his hands on them, the Holy Spirit came on them, and they spoke in tongues and prophesied.

Acts 19:2-6

And I will ask the Father, and he will give you another Counselor to be with you forever—the Spirit of truth.

The world cannot accept him, because it neither sees him nor knows him. But you know him, for he lives with you and will be in you.

John 14:16, 17

Don't you know that you yourselves are God's temple and that God's Spirit lives in you?

1 Corinthians 3:16

Do you not know that your body is a temple of the Holy Spirit, who is in you, whom you have received from God?

1 Corinthians 6:19

Because you are sons, God sent the Spirit of his Son into our hearts, the Spirit who calls out, "Abba, Father."

Galatians 4:6

We know that we live in him and he in us, because he has given us of his Spirit.

1 John 4:13

The Priority of Hungering and Seeking for God With All Your Heart

One thing I ask of the Lord, this is what I seek: that I may dwell in the house of the Lord all the days of my life, to gaze upon the beauty of the Lord and to seek him in his temple.

Psalm 27:4

My heart says of you, "Seek his face!" Your face, Lord, I will seek. Do not hide your face from me, do not turn your servant away in anger; you have been my helper. Do not reject me or forsake me, O God my Savior.

Psalm 27:8, 9

Fear the Lord, you his saints, for those who fear him lack nothing.

The lions may grow weak and hungry, but those who seek the Lord lack no good thing.

Psalm 34:9, 10

As the deer pants for streams of water, so my soul pants for you, O God.

My soul thirsts for God, for the living God. When can I go and meet with God?

Psalm 42:1, 2

Trust in him at all times, O people; pour out your hearts to him, for God is our refuge.

Selah Psalm 62:8

O God, you are my God, earnestly I seek you; my soul thirsts for you, my body longs for you, in a dry and weary land where there is no water.

I have seen you in the sanctuary and beheld your power and your glory.

Because your love is better than life, my lips will glorify you.

I will praise you as long as I live, and in your name I will lift up my hands.

Psalm 63:1-4

The poor will see and be glad —you who seek God, may your hearts live!

Psalm 69:32

Yet I am always with you; you hold me by my right hand.

You guide me with your counsel, and afterward you will take me into glory.

Whom have I in heaven but you? And earth has nothing I desire besides you.

My flesh and my heart may fail, but God is the strength of my heart and my portion forever.

Those who are far from you will perish; you destroy all who are unfaithful to you.

But as for me, it is good to be near God. I have made the Sovereign Lord my refuge; I will tell of all your deeds.

Psalm 73:23-28

My soul yearns, even faints, for the courts of the Lord; my heart and my flesh cry out for the living God.

Psalm 84:2

The Lord looks down from heaven on the sons of men to see if there are any who understand, any who seek God.

Psalm 14:2

He who has clean hands and a pure heart, who does not lift up his soul to an idol or swear by what is false.

He will receive blessing from the Lord and vindication from God his Savior.

Such is the generation of those who seek him, who seek your face, O God of Jacob.

Selah Psalm 24:4-6

Glory in his holy name; let the hearts of those who seek the Lord rejoice.

Look to the Lord and his strength; seek his face always.

Psalm 105:3, 4

Yes, Lord, walking in the way of your laws, we wait for you; your name and renown are the desire of our hearts.

My soul yearns for you in the night; in the morning my spirit longs for you. When your judgments come upon the earth, the people of the world learn righteousness.

Isaiah 26:8, 9

But whatever was to my profit I now consider loss for the sake of Christ.

What is more, I consider everything a loss compared to the surpassing greatness of knowing Christ Jesus my Lord, for whose sake I have lost all things. I consider them rubbish, that I may gain Christ

And be found in him, not having a righteousness of my own that comes from the law, but that which is through faith in Christ — the righteousness that comes from God and is by faith.

I want to know Christ and the power of his resurrection and the fellowship of sharing in his sufferings, becoming like him in his death,

And so, somehow, to attain to the resurrection from the dead.

Not that I have already obtained all this, or have already been made perfect, but I press on to take hold of that for which Christ Jesus took hold of me.

Philippians 3:7-12

Since, then, you have been raised with Christ, set your hearts on things above, where Christ is seated at the right hand of God.

Set your minds on things above, not on earthly things.

For you died, and your life is now hidden with Christ in God.

When Christ, who is your life, appears, then you also will appear with him in glory.

Colossians 3:1-4

But seek first his kingdom and his righteousness, and all these things will be given to you as well.

Matthew 6:33

Come near to Go4and he will come near to you. Wash your hands, you sinners, and purify your hearts, you double-minded.

James 4:8

Love the Lord your God with all your heart and with all your soul and with all your strength.

Deuteronomy 6:5

So be very careful to love the Lord your God.

Joshua 23:11

I seek you with all my heart; do not let me stray from your commands.

Psalm 119:10

The Priority of Obedience to God

Now if you obey me fully and keep my covenant, then out of all nations you will be my treasured possession. Although the whole earth is mine, you will be for me a kingdom of priests and a holy nation.

Exodus 19:5, 6a

And if you walk in my ways and obey my statutes and commands as David your father did, I will give you a long life.

1 King 3:14

Blessed is the man who does not walk in the counsel of the wicked or stand in the way of sinners or sit in the seat of mockers.

But his delight is in the law of the Lord, and on his law he meditates day and night.

Psalm 1:1, 2

All the ways of the Lord are loving and faithful for those who keep the demands of his covenant.

Psalm 25:10

The fear of the Lord is the beginning of wisdom; all who follow his precepts have good understanding. To him belongs eternal praise.

Psalm 111:10

If you are willing and obedient, you will eat the best from the land.

Isaiah 1:19

Anyone who breaks one of the least of these commandments and teaches others to do the same will be called least in the kingdom of heaven, but whoever practices and teaches these commands will be called great in the kingdom of heaven.

Matthew 5:19

For whoever does the will Of my Father in heaven is my brother and sister and mother.

Matthew 12:50

If you love me, you will obey what I command.

Jesus replied, "If anyone loves me, he will obey my teaching. My Father will love him, and we will come to him and make our home with him."

John 14:15, 23

If you obey my commands, you will remain in my love, just as I have obeyed my Father's commands and remain in his love.

You are my friends if you do what I command.

John 15:10, 14

And receive from him anything we ask, because we obey his commands and do what pleases him.

1 John 3:22

The Priority of God's Word

Do not let this Book of the Law depart from your mouth; meditate on it day and night, so that you may be careful to do everything written in it. Then you will be prosperous and successful.

Joshua 1:8

All Scripture is God-breathed and is useful for teaching, rebuking, correcting and training in righteousness.

2 Timothy 3:16

Heaven and earth will pass away, but my words will never pass away.

Mark 13:31

Jesus answered, "It is written: 'Man does not live on bread alone, but on every word that comes from the mouth of God.'"

Matthew 4:4

For the word of God is living and active. Sharper than any double-edged sword, it penetrates even to dividing soul and spirit, joints and marrow; it judges the thoughts and attitudes of the heart.

Hebrews 4:12

For prophecy never had its origin in the will of man, but men spoke from God as they were carried along by the Holy Spirit.

2 Peter 1:21

But his delight is in the law of the Lord, and on his law he meditates day and night.

Psalm 1:2

Your word is a lamp to my feet and a light for my path.

Psalm 119:105

He sent forth his word and healed them; he rescued them from the grave.

Psalm 107:20

Like newborn babies, crave pure spiritual milk, so that by it you may grow up in your salvation.

1 Peter 2:2

Do not merely listen to the word, and so deceive yourselves. Do what it says.

James 1:22

To the Jews who had believed him, Jesus said, "If you hold to my teaching, you are really my disciples.

"Then you will know the truth, and the truth will set you free."

John 8:31, 32

17

Consequently, faith comes from hearing the message, and the message is heard through the word of Christ.

Romans 10:17

But the word of the Lord stands forever. And this is the word that was preached to you.

1 Peter 1:25

He remembers his covenant forever, the word he commanded, for a thousand generations,

1 Chronicles 16:15

When I am afraid, I will trust in you.

In God, whose word I praise, in God I trust; I will not be afraid. What can mortal man do to me?

Psalm 56:3, 4

For everything that was written in the past was written to teach us, so that through endurance and the encouragement of the Scriptures we might have hope.

Romans 15:4

The Priority of Prayer

If my people, who are called by my name, will humble themselves and pray and seek my face and turn from their wicked ways, then will I hear from heaven and will forgive their sin and will heal their land.

2 Chronicles 7:14

My heart says of you, "Seek his face!*' Your face, Lord, I will seek.

Psalm 27:8

Ask and it will be given to you; seek and you will find; knock and the door will be opened to you.

For everyone who asks receives; he who seeks finds; and to him who knocks, the door will be opened.

Matthew 7:7, 8

"Have faith in God," Jesus answered.

"I tell you the truth, if anyone says to this mountain, 'Go, throw yourself into the sea,' and does not doubt in his heart but believes that what he says will happen, it will be done for him.

"Therefore I tell you, whatever you ask in prayer, believe that you have received it, and it will be yours."

Mark 11:22-24

Do not be anxious about anything, but in everything, by prayer and petition, with thanksgiving, present your requests to God.

Philippians 4:6

If you remain in me and my words remain in you, ask whatever you wish, and it will be given you.

John 15:7

And I will do whatever you ask in my name, so that

the Son may bring glory to the Father. You may ask me for anything in my name, and I will do it.

John 14:13, 14

In that day you will no longer ask me anything. I tell you the truth, my Father will give you whatever you ask in my name.

Until now you have not asked for anything in my name. Ask and you will receive, and your joy will be complete.

John 16:23, 24

But you, dear friends, build yourselves up in your most holy faith and pray in the Holy Spirit.

Jude 20

This is the confidence we have in approaching God: that if we ask anything according to his will, he hears us.

And if we know that he hears us — whatever we ask — we know that we have what we asked of him.

1 John 5:14, 15

Let us then approach the throne of grace with confidence, so that we may receive mercy and find grace to help us in our time of need.

Hebrews 4:16

Therefore confess your sins to each other and pray for each other so that you may be healed. The prayer of a righteous man is powerful and effective.

James 5:16

The eyes of the Lord are on the righteous and his ears are attentive to their cry.

Psalm 34:15

Call to me and I will answer you and tell you great and unsearchable things you do not know.

Jeremiah 33:3

Again, I tell you that if two of you on earth agree about anything you ask for, it will be done for you by my Father in heaven.

Matthew 18:19

If you believe, you will receive whatever you ask for in prayer.

Matthew 21:22

The Priority of Praise and Worship

Let them give thanks to the Lord for his unfailing love and his wonderful deeds for men,

For he satisfies the thirsty and fills the hungry with good things.

Psalm 107:8, 9

Offer right sacrifices and trust in the Lord. Psalm 4:5

I will praise you, O Lord, with all my heart; I will tell of all your wonders.

I will be glad and rejoice in you; I will sing praise to your name, O Most High.

Psalm 9:1, 2

Be exalted, O Lord, in your strength; we will sing and praise your might.

Psalm 21:13

Love the Lord, all his saints! The Lord preserves the faithful, but the proud he pays back in full.

Be strong and take heart, all you who hope in the Lord.

Psalm 31:23, 24

Sing joyfully to the Lord, you righteous; it is fitting for the upright to praise him.

Praise the Lord with the harp; make music to him on the ten-stringed lyre.

Sing to him a new song; play skillfully, and shout for joy.

Psalm 33:1-3

I will extol the Lord at all times; his praise will always be on my lips.

My soul will boast in the Lord; let the afflicted hear and rejoice.

Glorify the Lord with me; let us exalt his name together.

Psalm 34:1-3

He who sacrifices thank offerings honors me, and he prepares the way so that I may show him the salvation of God.

Psalm 50:23

Come, let us sing for joy to the Lord; let us shout aloud to the Rock of our salvation.

Let us come before him with thanksgiving and extol him with music and song.

For the Lord is the great God, the great King above all gods.

Psalm 95:1-3

Rejoice in the Lord always. I will say it again: Rejoice!

Philippians 4:4

"Shout and be glad, O Daughter of Zion. For I am coming, and I will live among you," declares the Lord.

Zechariah 2:10

And let us consider how we may spur one another on toward love and good deeds.

Let us not give up meeting together, as some are in the habit of doing, but let us encourage one another—and all the more as you see the Day approaching.

Hebrews 10:24, 25

The Priority of Attending Your Local Church

Though one may be overpowered, two can defend themselves. A cord of three strands is not quickly broken,

Ecclesiastes 4:12

How good and pleasant it is when brothers live together in unity!

Psalm 133:1

Make every effort to keep the unity of the Spirit through the bond of peace.

Ephesians 4:3

Until we all reach unity in the faith and in the knowledge of the Son of God and become mature, attaining to the whole measure of the fullness of Christ.

Ephesians 4:13

You also, like living stones, are being built into a spiritual house to be a holy priest hood, offering spiritual sacrifices acceptable to God through Jesus Christ.

1 Peter2:5

Those who accepted his message were baptized, and about three thousand were added to their number that day.

They devoted themselves to the apostles' teaching and to the fellowship, to the breaking of bread and to prayer.

Acts 2:41, 42

Every day they continued to meet together in the temple courts. They broke bread in their homes and ate together with glad and sincere hearts,

Praising God and enjoying the favor of all the people. And the Lord added to their number daily those who were being saved.

Acts 2:46, 47

For where two or three come together in my name, there am I with them.

Matthew 18:20

Just as each of us has one body with many members, and these members do not all have the same function,

So in Christ we who are many form one body, and each member belongs to all the others.

Romans 12:4, 5

The body is a unit, though it is made up of many parts; and though all its parts are many, they form one body. So it is with Christ.

For we were all baptized by one Spirit into one body —whether Jews or Greeks, slave or free —and we were all given the one Spirit to drink.

Now the body is not made up of one part but of many.

1 Corinthians 12:12-14

But in fact God has arranged the parts in the body, every one of them, just as he wanted them to be.

If they were all one part, where would the body be?

As it is, there are many parts, but one body.

1 Corinthians 12:18-20

And in the church God has appointed first of all apostles, second prophets, third teachers, then workers of miracles, also those having gifts of healing, those able to help others, those with gifts of administration, and those speaking in different kinds of tongues.

1 Corinthians 12:28

Praise the Lord. I will extol the Lord with all my heart in the council of the upright and in the assembly.

Psalm 111:1

The Priority of Witnessing and Spreading the Gospel

You are the light of the world. A city on a hill cannot be hidden.

Neither do people light a lamp and put it under a bowl. Instead they put it on its stand, and it gives light to everyone in the house.

In the same way, let your light shine before men, that they may see your good deeds and praise your Father in heaven.

Matthew 5:14-16

For Christ did not send me to baptize, but to preach the gospel —not with words of human wisdom, lest the cross of Christ be emptied of its power.

For the message of the cross is foolishness to those who are perishing, but to us who are being saved it is the power of God.

For it is written: "I will destroy the wisdom of the wise; the intelligence of the intelligent I will frustrate."

Where is the wise man? Where is the scholar? Where is the philosopher of this age? Has not God made foolish the wisdom of the world?

For since in the wisdom of God the world through its wisdom did not know him, God was pleased through the foolishness of what was preached to save those who believe.

Jews demand miraculous signs and Greeks look for wisdom,

But we preach Christ crucified: a stumbling block to Jews and foolishness to Gentiles,

But to those whom God has called, both Jews and Greeks, Christ the power of God and the wisdom of God.

For the foolishness of God is wiser than man's wisdom, and the weakness of God is stronger than man's strength.

Brothers, think of what you were when you were called. Not many of you were wise by human standards; not many were influential; not many were of noble birth.

But God chose the foolish things of the world to shame the wise; God chose the weak things of the world to shame the strong.

He chose the lowly things of this world and the despised things —and the things that are not —to nullify the things that are,

So that no one may boast before him.

1 Corinthians 1:17-29

When I came to you, brothers, I did not come with eloquence or superior wisdom as I proclaimed to you the testimony about God.

For I resolved to know nothing while I was with you except Jesus Christ and him crucified.

I came to you in weakness and fear, and with much trembling.

My message and my preaching were not with wise and persuasive words, but with a demonstration of the Spirit's power,

So that your faith might not rest on men's wisdom, but on God's power.

1 Corinthians 2:1-5

But thanks be to God, who always leads us in triumphal procession in Christ and through us spreads everywhere the fragrance of the knowledge of him.

2 Corinthians 2:14

To the one we are the smell of death; to the other, the fragrance of life. And who is equal to such a task?

2 Corinthians 2:16

The mystery that has been kept hidden for ages and generations, but is now disclosed to the saints.

To them God has chosen to make known among the Gentiles the glorious riches of this mystery, which is Christ in you, the hope of glory.

We proclaim him, admonishing and teaching everyone with all wisdom, so that we may present everyone perfect in Christ.

To this end I labor, struggling with all his energy, which so powerfully works in me.

Colossians 1:26-29

Do your best to present yourself to God as one approved, a workman who does not need to be ashamed and who correctly handles the word of truth.

2 Timothy 2:15

So that you may become blameless and pure, children of God without fault in a crooked and depraved generation, in which you shine like stars in the universe.

Philippians 2:15

And teaching them to obey everything I have commanded you. And surely I am with you always, to the very end of the age.

Matthew 28:20

He said to them, "Go into all the world and preach the good news to all creation."

Mark 16:15

By this all men will know that you are my disciples, if you love one another.

John 13:35

All this is from God, who reconciled us to himself through Christ and gave us the ministry of reconciliation.

2 Corinthians 5:18

We are therefore Christ's ambassadors, as though God were making his appeal through us. We implore you on Christ's behalf: Be reconciled to God.

2 Corinthians 5:20

But you are a chosen people, a royal priesthood, a holy nation, a people belonging to God, that you may declare the praises of him who called you out of darkness into his wonderful light.

1 Peter 2:9

And this gospel of the kingdom will be preached in the whole world as a testimony to all nations, and then the end will come.

Matthew 24:14

The Spirit of the Sovereign Lord is on me, because the Lord has anointed me to preach good news to the poor. He has sent me to bind up the brokenhearted, to proclaim freedom for the captives and release from darkness for the prisoners.

Isaiah 61:1

Pray also for me, that whenever I open my mouth, words may be given me so that I will fearlessly make known the mystery of the gospel.

Ephesians 6:19

I am not ashamed of the gospel, because it is the power of God for the salvation of everyone who believes: first for the Jew, then for the Gentile.

For in the gospel a righteousness from God is revealed, a righteousness that is by faith from first to last, just as it is written: 'The righteous will live by faith.'

Romans 1:16, 11

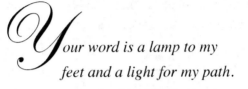

our word is a lamp to my feet and a light for my path.

_____

Psalm 119:105

When You Want To Be...

When You Want To Be Patient

Be still before the Lord and wait patiently for him; do not fret when men succeed in their ways, when they carry out their wicked schemes.

Psalm 37:7

I waited patiently for the Lord; he turned to me and heard my cry.

Psalm 40:1

For you have been my hope, O Sovereign Lord, my confidence since my youth.

Psalm 71:5

The end of a matter is better than its beginning, and patience is better than pride.

Do not be quickly provoked in your spirit, for anger resides in the lap of fools.

Ecclesiastes 7:8, 9

But those who hope in the Lord will renew their strength. They will soar on wings like eagles; they will run and not grow weary, they will walk and not be faint.

Isaiah 40:31

But blessed is the man who trusts in the Lord, whose confidence is in him.

Jeremiah 17:7

By standing firm you will gain life.

Luke 21:19

Not only so, but we also rejoice in our sufferings, because we know that suffering produces perseverance;

Perseverance, character; and character, hope.

And hope does not disappoint us, because God has poured out his love into our hearts by the Holy Spirit, whom he has given us.

Romans 5:3-5

But if we hope for what we do not yet have, we wait for it patiently.

Romans 8:25

For everything that was written in the past was written to teach us, so that through endurance and the encouragement of the Scriptures we might have hope.

May the God who gives endurance and encouragement give you a spirit of unity among yourselves as you follow Christ Jesus.

May the God of hope fill you with all joy and peace as you trust in him, so that you may overflow with hope by the power of the Holy Spirit.

Romans 15:4, 5, 13

But the fruit of the Spirit is love, joy, peace, patience, kindness, goodness, faithfulness, gentleness and self-control.

Galatians 5:22, 23a

I can do everything through him who gives me strength.

Philippians 4:13

We do not want you to become lazy, but to imitate those who through faith and patience inherit what has been promised.

Hebrews 6:12

So do not throw away your confidence; it will be richly rewarded.

You need to persevere so that when you have done the will of God, you will receive what he has promised.

For in just a very little while, He who is coming will come and will not delay.

Hebrews 10:35-37

Because you know that the testing of your faith develops perseverance.

Perseverance must finish its work so that you maybe mature and complete, not lacking anything.

James 1:3, 4

Be patient, then, brothers, until the Lord's coming. See how the farmer waits for the land to yield its valuable crop and how patient he is for the autumn and spring rains.

You too, be patient and stand firm, because the Lord's coming is near.

James 5:7, 8

For this very reason, make every effort to add to your faith goodness; and to goodness, knowledge;

And to knowledge, self-control; and to self-control, perseverance; and to perseverance, godliness.

2 Peter 1:5, 6

When You Want To Be Loving

Hatred stirs up dissension, but love covers over all wrongs.

Proverbs 10:12

Many waters cannot quench love; rivers cannot wash it away. If one were to give all the wealth of his house for love, it would be utterly scorned.

Song of Songs 8:7

A new command I give you: Love one another. As I have loved you, so you must love one another.

By this all men will know that you are my disciples, if you love one another.

John 13:34, 35

As the Father has loved me, so have I loved you. Now remain in my love.

If you obey my commands, you will remain in my love, just as I have obeyed my Father's commands and remain in his love.

My command is this: Love each other as I have loved you.

Greater love has no one than this, that he lay down his life for his friends.

You are my friends if you do what I command.

I no longer call you servants, because a servant does not know his master's business. Instead, I have called you friends, for everything that I learned from my Father I have made known to you.

You did not choose me, but I chose you and appointed you to go and bear fruit — fruit that will last. Then the Father will give you whatever you ask in my name.

This is my command: Love each other.

John 15:9, 10, 12-17

Let no debt remain outstanding, except the continuing debt to love one another, for he who loves his fellowman has fulfilled the law.

Love does no harm to its neighbor. Therefore love is the fulfillment of the law.

Romans 13:8, 10

If I speak in the tongues of men and of angels, but have not love, I am only a resounding gong or a clanging cymbal.

If I have the gift of prophecy and can fathom all mysteries and all knowledge, and if I have a faith that can move mountains, but have not love, I am nothing.

If I give all I possess to the poor and surrender my body to the flames, but have not love, I gain nothing.

Love is patient, love is kind. It does not envy, it does not boast, it is not proud.

It is not rude, it is not self-seeking, it is not easily angered, it keeps no record of wrongs.

Love does not delight in evil but rejoices with the truth.

It always protects, always trusts, always hopes, always perseveres. Love never fails.

1 Corinthians 13:1-8a

And now these three remain: faith, hope and love. But the greatest of these is love.

1 Corinthians 13:13

And live a life of love,just as Christ loved us and gave himself up for us as a fragrant offering and sacrifice to God.

Ephesians 5:2

May the Lord make your love increase and overflow for each other and for everyone else, just as ours does for you.

1 Thessalonians 3:12

God is not unjust; he will not forget your work and the love you have shown him as you have helped his people and continue to help them.

Hebrews 6:10

And let us consider how we may spur one another on toward love and good deeds.

Hebrews 10:24

If you really keep the royal law found in Scripture, "Love your neighbor as yourself," you are doing right.

James 2:8

This is the message you heard from the beginning: We should love one another. 1 John 3:11 We know that we have passed from death to life, because we love our brothers. Anyone who does not love remains in death.

1 John 3:14

Dear children, let us not love with words or tongue but with actions and in truth.

1 John 3:18

Dear friends, let us love one another, for love comes from God. Everyone who loves has been born of God and knows God.

Whoever does not love does not know God, because God is love.

1 John 4:7, 8

Above all, love each other deeply, because love covers over a multitude of sins.

1 Peter 4:8

When You Want To Be Giving

"Bring the whole tithe into the store house, that there may be food in my house. Test me in this," says the Lord Almighty, "and see if I will not throw open the floodgates of heaven and pour out so much blessing that you will not have room enough for it.

"I will prevent pests from devouring your crops, and the vines in your fields will not cast their fruit," says the Lord Almighty.

"Then all the nations will call you blessed, for yours will be a delightful land," says the Lord Almighty."

Malachi 3:10-12

But as for you, be strong and do not give up, for your work will be rewarded.

2 Chronicles 15:7

Good will come to him who is generous and lends freely, who conducts his affairs with justice.

Psalm 112:5

Honor the Lord with your wealth, with the first fruits of all your crops;

Then your barns will be filled to overflowing, and your vats will brim over with new wine. . . :

Proverbs 3:9,10

He who is kind to the poor lends to the Lord, and he will reward him for what he has done.

Proverbs 19:17

A generous man will himself be blessed, for he shares his food with the poor.

Proverbs 22:9

He who gives to the poor will lack nothing, but he who closes his eyes to them receives many curses.

Proverbs 28:27

Cast your bread upon the waters, for after many days you will find it again.

Ecclesiastes 11:1

Heal the sick, raise the dead, cleanse those who have leprosy, drive out demons. Freely you have received, freely give.

Matthew 10:8

And everyone who has left houses or brothers or sisters or father or mother or children or fields for my sake will receive a hundred times as much and will inherit eternal life.

Matthew 19:29

Give, and it will be given to you. A good measure, pressed

down, shaken together and running over, will be poured into your lap. For with the measure you use, it will be measured to you.

Luke 6:38

On the first day of every week, each one of you should set aside a sum of money in keeping with his income, saving it up, so that when I come no collections will have to be made.

7 Corinthians 16:2

Remember this: Who ever sows sparingly will also reap sparingly, and whoever sows generously will also reap generously.

Each man should give what he has decided in his heart to give, not reluctantly or under compulsion, for God loves a cheerful giver.

And God is able to make all grace abound to you, so that in all things at all times, having all that you need, you will abound in every good work.

2 Corinthians 9:6-8

Command those who are rich in this present world not to be arrogant nor to put their hope in wealth, which is so uncertain, but to put their hope in God, who richly provides us with everything for our enjoyment.

Command them to do good, to be rich in good deeds, and to be generous and willing to share.

In this way they will lay up treasure for themselves as a firm foundation for the coming age, so that they may take hold of the life that is truly life.

Timothy 6:17-19

If anyone has material possessions and sees his brother in need but has no pity on him, how can the love of God be in him?

Dear children, let us not love with words or tongue but with actions and in truth.

John 3:17, 18

Dear friend, I pray that you may enjoy good health and that all may go well with you, even as your soul is getting along well.

3 John 2

When You Want To Be Godly

He did what was right in the eyes of the Lord, just as his father David had done.

2 Chronicles 29:2

He who walks with the wise grows wise, but a companion of fools suffers harm.

Proverbs 13:20

And if anyone gives even a cup of cold water to one

of these little ones because he is my disciple, I tell you the truth, he will certainly not lose his reward.

Matthew 10:42

Just as the Son of Man did not come to be served, but to serve, and to give his life as a ransom for many.

Matthew 20:28

Not so with you. Instead, whoever wants to become great among you must be your servant,

And whoever wants to be first must be slave of all.

Mark 10:43, 44

The expert in the law replied, "The one who had mercy on him." Jesus told him, "Go and do likewise."

Luke 10:37

I have set you an example that you should do as I have done for you.

I tell you the truth, no servant is greater than his master, nor is a messenger greater than the one who sent him.

A new command I give you: Love one another. As I have loved you, so you must love one another.

John 13:15, 16, 34

May the God who gives endurance and encouragement give you a spirit of unity among yourselves as you follow Christ Jesus,

So that with one heart and mouth you may glorify the God and Father of our Lord Jesus Christ.

Accept one another, then, just as Christ accepted you, in order to bring praise to God.

Romans 15:5-7

Now it is required that those who have been given a trust must prove faithful.

1 Corinthians 4:2

Therefore, my dear brothers, stand firm. Let nothing move you. Always give yourselves fully to the work of the Lord, because you know that your labor in the Lord is not in vain.

1 Corinthians 15:58

Carry each other's burdens, and in this way you will fulfill the law of Christ.

Therefore, as we have opportunity, let us do good to all people, especially to those who belong to the family of believers.

Galatians 6:2, 10

Be imitators of God, therefore, as dearly loved children

And live a life of love, just as Christ loved us and gave himself up for us as a fragrant offering and sacrifice to God.

Ephesians 5:1, 2

Slaves, obey your earthly masters with respect and fear,

and with sincerity of heart, just as you would obey Christ.

Obey them not only to win their favor when their eye is on you, but like slaves of Christ, doing the will of God from your heart.

Serve wholeheartedly, as if you were serving the Lord, not men.

Ephesians 6:5-7

Your attitude should be the same as that of Christ Jesus:

Who, being in very nature God, did not consider equality with God something to be grasped,

But made himself nothing, taking the very nature of a servant, being made in human likeness.

And being found in appearance as a man, he humbled himself and became obedient to death —even death on a cross!

Philippians 2:5-8

Bear with each other and forgive whatever grievances you may have against one another. Forgive as the Lord forgave you.

Slaves, obey your earthly masters in everything; and do it, not only when their eye is on you and to win their favor, but with sincerity of heart and reverence for the Lord.

Colossians 3:13, 22

To this you were called, because Christ suffered for you,

leaving you an example, that you should follow in his steps.

1 Peter 2:21

For everything in the world —the cravings of sinful man, the lust of his eyes and the boasting of what he has and does — comes not from the Father but from the world.

1 John 2:16

This is how we know what love is: Jesus Christ laid down his life for us. And we ought to lay down our lives for our brothers.

1 John 3:16

When You Want To Be Diligent

But as for you, be strong and do not give up, for your work will be rewarded.

2 Chronicles 15:7

And who knows but that you have come to royal position for such a time as this?

Esther 4:14b

He who gathers crops in summer is a wise son, but he who sleeps during harvest is a disgraceful son.

Proverbs 10:5

Diligent hands will rule, but laziness ends in slave labor.

Proverbs 12:24

The sluggard craves and gets nothing, but the desires of

the diligent are fully satisfied.

Proverbs 13:4

The plans of the diligent lead to profit as surely as haste leads to poverty.

Proverbs 21:5

Do you see a man skilled in his work? He will serve before kings; he will not serve before obscure men.

Proverbs 22:29

The Sovereign Lord is my strength; he makes my feet like the feet of a deer, he enables me to go on the heights. For the

Do you not say, "Four months more and then the harvest?" I tell you, open your eyes and look at the fields! They are ripe for harvest.

John 4:35

As long as it is day, we must do the work of him who sent me. Night is coming, when no one can work.

John 9:4

Therefore, as we have opportunity, let us do good to all people, especially to those who belong to the family of believers.

Galatians 6:10

Now to him who is able to do immeasurably more than

all we ask or imagine, according to his power that is at work within us.

Ephesians 3:20

I can do everything through him who gives me strength.

Philippians 4:13

We want each of you to show this same diligence to the very end, in order to make your hope sure.

Hebrews 6:11

If any of you lacks wisdom, he should ask God, who gives generously to all without finding fault, and it will be given to him.

James 1:5

So then, dear friends, since you are looking forward to this, make every effort to be found spotless, blameless and at peace with him.

2 Peter 3:8

I know your deeds. See, I have placed before you an open door that no one can shut.

I know that you have little strength, yet you have kept my word and have not denied my name.

Revelation 3:8

When You Want To Be Honest

Now if you obey me fully and keep my covenant, then out

of all nations you will be my treasured possession. Although the whole earth is mine, you will be for me a kingdom of priests and a holy nation.

Exodus 19:5, 6a

And if you walk in my ways and obey my statutes and commands as David your father did, I will give you a long life.

1 Kings 3:14

Then the Lord said to Satan, "Have you considered my servant Job? There is no one on earth like him; he is blameless and upright, a man who fears God and shuns evil. And he still maintains his integrity, though you incited me against him to ruin him without any reason."

Job 2:3

Blessed is the man who does not walk in the counsel of the wicked or stand in the way of sinners or sit in the seat of mockers.

But his delight is in the law of the Lord, and on his law he meditates day and night.

Psalm 1:1, 2

All the ways of the Lord are loving and faithful for those who keep the demands of his covenant.

Psalm 25:10

The fear of the Lord is the beginning of wisdom; all who follow his precepts have good understanding. To him

49

belongs eternal praise.

Psalm 111:10

Blessed are they who keep his statutes and seek him with all their heart.

You have laid down precepts that are to be fully obeyed.

Psalm 119:2, 4

Vindicate me, 0 Lord, for I have led a blameless life; I have trusted in the Lord without wavering.

Psalm 26:1

In my integrity you uphold me and set me in your presence forever.

Psalm 41:12

And David shepherded them with integrity of heart; with skillful hands he led them.

Psalm 78:72

The integrity of the upright guides them, but the unfaithful are destroyed by their duplicity.

Proverbs 11:3

Better a poor man whose walk is blame less than a fool whose lips are perverse.

He who obeys instructions guards his life, but he who is contemptuous of his ways will die.

Proverbs 19:1, 16

The righteous man leads a blameless life; blessed are his children after him.

Proverbs 20:7

If you are willing and obedient, you will eat the best from the land.

Isaiah 1:19

Do not repay anyone evil for evil. Be careful to do what is right in the eyes of everybody.

Romans 12:17

Finally, brothers, whatever is true, what ever is noble, whatever is right, whatever is pure, whatever is lovely, whatever is admirable —if anything is excellent or praiseworthy —think about such things.

Philippians 4:8

Live such good lives among the pagans that, though they accuse you of doing wrong, they may see your good deeds and glorify God on the day he visits us.

1 Peter 2:12

When You Want To Be Understanding

Trust in the Lord with all your heart and lean not on your own understanding;

In all your ways acknowledge him, and he will make your paths straight.

Proverbs 3:5, 6

As for God, his way is perfect; the word of the Lord is flawless. He is a shield for all who take refuge in him.

Psalm 18:30

Teach me your way, O Lord; lead me in a straight path because of my oppressors.

Psalm 27:11

I am your servant; give me discernment that I may understand your statutes.

The unfolding of your words gives light; it gives understanding to the simple.

May my cry come before you, O Lord; give me understanding according to your word.

Psalm 119:125, 130, 169

Counsel and sound judgment are mine; I have understanding and power.

Proverbs 8:14

Understanding is a fountain of life to those who have it, but folly brings punishment to fools.

A wise man's heart guides his mouth, and his lips promote instruction.

Proverbs 16:22, 23

By wisdom a house is built, and through understanding it is established;

Through knowledge its rooms are filled with rare and beautiful treasures.

Proverbs 24:3, 4

"For my thoughts are not your thoughts, neither are your ways my ways," declares the Lord.

"As the heavens are higher than the earth, so are my ways higher than your ways and my thoughts than your thoughts."

Isaiah 55:8, 9

Call to me and I will answer you and tell you great and unsearchable things you do not know.

Jeremiah 33:3

Then he opened their minds so they could understand the Scriptures.

Luke 24:45

Because through Christ Jesus the law of the Spirit of life sets me free from the law of sin and death.

Romans 8:2

I keep asking that the God of our Lord Jesus Christ, the glorious Father, may give you the Spirit of wisdom and revelation, so that you may know him better.

I pray also that the eyes of your heart may be enlightened in order that you may know the hope to which he has called you, the riches of his glorious inheritance in the saints.

Ephesians 1:17, 18

Therefore do not be foolish, but under stand what the Lord's will is.

Ephesians 5:17

We know also that the Son of God has come and has given us understanding, so that we may know him who is true. And we are in him who is true —even in his Son Jesus Christ. He is the true God and eternal life.

1 John 5:20

When You Want To Be Joyful Let the heavens rejoice, let the earth be glad; let them say among the nations, "The Lord reigns!"

Chronicles 16:31

You have filled my heart with greater joy than when their grain and new wine abound.

Psalm 4:7

But let all who take refuge in you be glad; let them ever sing for joy. Spread your protection over them, that those who love your name may rejoice in you.

Psalm 5:11

Weeping may remain for a night, but rejoicing comes in the morning.

Psalm 30:5b

When You Want To Be Joyful

Delight yourself in the Lord and he will give you the desires of your heart.

Psalm 37:4

Blessed are those who have learned to acclaim you, who walk in the light of your presence, O Lord.

Psalm 89:15

Shout for joy to the Lord, all the earth.

Worship the Lord with gladness; come before him With joyful songs. Know that the Lord is God. It is he who made us, and we are his; we are his people, the sheep of his pasture. Enter his gates with thanksgiving and his courts with praise; give thanks to him and praise his name.

Psalm 100:1-4

Those who sow in tears will reap with songs of joy.

Psalm 126:5

A happy heart makes the face cheerful, but heartache crushes the spirit.

Proverbs 15:13

A cheerful heart is good medicine, but a crushed spirit dries up the bones.

Proverbs 17:22

You will go out in joy and be led forth in peace; the

mountains and hills will burst into song before you, and all the trees of the field will clap their hands.

Isaiah 55:12

Though the fig tree does not bud and there are no grapes on the vines, though the olive crop fails and the fields produce no food, though there are no sheep in the pen and no cattle in the stalls, Yet I will rejoice in the Lord, I will be joyful in God my Savior.

Habakkuk 3:17, 18

However, do not rejoice that the spirits submit to you, but rejoice that your names are written in heaven.

Luke 10:20

May the God of hope fill you with all joy and peace as you trust in him, so that you may overflow with hope by the power of the Holy Spirit.

Romans 15:13

But the fruit of the Spirit is love, joy, peace, patience, kindness, goodness, faithfulness, gentleness and self-control.

Galatians 5:22, 23a

Speak to one another with psalms, hymns and spiritual songs. Sing and make music in your heart to the Lord.

Ephesians 5:19

We write this to make our joy complete.

7 John 1:4

When You Want To Be Courageous

Be strong and courageous. Do not be afraid or terrified because of them, for the Lord your God goes with you; he will never leave you nor forsake you.

Deuteronomy 31:6

Be strong and courageous, for you will bring the Israelites into the land I promised them on oath, and I myself will be with you.

Deuteronomy 31:23b

Be strong and courageous, because you will lead these people to inherit the land I swore to their forefathers to give them.

Joshua 1:6

David also said to Solomon his son, "Be strong and courageous, and do the work. Do not be afraid or discouraged, for the Lord God, my God, is with you. He will not fail you or forsake you until all the work for the service of the temple of the Lord is finished.

Chronicles 28:20

But as for you, be strong and do not give up, for your work will be rewarded.

2 Chronicles 15:7

Be strong and take heart, all you who hope in the Lord.

Psalm 31:24

Counsel and sound judgment are mine; I have understanding and power.

Proverbs 8:14

Strengthen the feeble hands, steady the knees that give way.

Isaiah 35:3

So do not fear, for I am with you; do not be dismayed, for I am your God. I will strengthen you and help you; I will uphold you with my righteous right hand.

Isaiah 41:10

The Sovereign Lord is my strength-he makes my feet like the feet of a deer, he enables me to go on the heights. For the director of music. On my stringed instruments.

Habakkuk 3:19

But you will receive power when the Holy Spirit comes on you; and you will be my witnesses in Jerusalem, and in all Judea and Samaria, and to the ends of the earth.

Acts 1:8

But God chose the foolish things of the world to shame the wise; God chose the weak things of the world to shame the strong.

1 Corinthians 1:27

To one there is given through the Spirit the message of wisdom, to another the message of knowledge by means of the same Spirit.

1 Corinthians 12:8

And God is able to make all grace abound to you, so that in all things at all times, having all that you need, you will abound in every good work.

2 Corinthians 9:8

Now to him who is able to do immeasurably more than all we ask or imagine, according to his power that is at work within us.

Ephesians 3:20

I can do everything through him who gives me strength.

Philippians 4:13

So do not throw away your confidence; it will be richly rewarded.

You need to persevere so that when you have done the will of God, you will receive what he has promised.

Hebrews 10:35, 36

If any of you lacks wisdom, he should ask God, who gives generously to all without finding fault, and it will be given to him.

James 1:5

When You Want To Be Compassionate

Then you will call, and the Lord will answer; you will cry for help, and he will say: Here am I. If you do away with the yoke of oppression, with the pointing finger and malicious talk,

And if you spend yourselves in behalf of the hungry and satisfy the needs of the oppressed, then your light will rise in the darkness, and your night will become like the noonday.

The Lord will guide you always; he will satisfy your needs in a sun-scorched land and will strengthen your frame. You will be like a well-watered garden, like a spring whose waters never fail.

Isaiah 58:9-11

The Lord is my shepherd, I shall not be in want.

Psalm 23:1

All the ways of the Lord are loving and faithful for those who keep the demands of his covenant.

Psalm 25:10

The wicked borrow and do not repay, but the righteous give generously.

Psalm 37:21

Yet he was merciful; he forgave their iniquities and did not destroy them. Time after time he restrained his anger and did not stir up his full wrath.

Psalm 78:38

He who pursues righteousness and love finds life, prosperity and honor.

Proverbs 21:21

He who conceals his sins does not prosper, but whoever confesses and renounces them finds mercy.

Proverbs 28:13

Can a mother forget the baby at her breast and have no compassion on the child she has borne? Though she may forget, I will not forget you!

Isaiah 49:15

But after I uproot them, I will again have compassion and will bring each of them back to his own inheritance and his own country.

Jeremiah 12:15

When Jesus landed and saw a large crowd, he had compassion on them, because they were like sheep without a shepherd. So he began teaching them many things.

Mark 6:34

As he approached the town gate, a dead person was being carried out —the only son of his mother, and she was a widow. And a large crowd from the town was with her.

When the Lord saw her, his heart went out to her and he said, "Don't cry."

Luke 7:12, 13

Love is patient, love is kind. It does not envy, it does not boast, it is not proud.

It is not rude, it is not self-seeking, it is not easily angered, it keeps no record of wrongs.

Love does not delight in evil but rejoices with the truth.

It always protects, always trusts, always hopes, always perseveres.

1 Corinthians 13:4-7

Finally, all of you, live in harmony with one another; be sympathetic, love as brothers, be compassionate and humble.

1 Peter 3:8

When You Want To Be Consistent

I the Lord do not change.

Malachi 3:6a

I will establish his kingdom forever if he is unswerving in carrying out my commands and laws, as is being done at this time.

1 Chronicles 28:7

But you are a shield around me, O Lord; you bestow glory on me and lift up my head.

Psalm 3:3

The Lord is my light and my salvation — whom shall I

fear? The Lord is the stronghold of my life —of whom shall I be afraid?

Though an army besiege me, my heart will not fear; though war break out against me, even then will I be confident.

For in the day of trouble he will keep me safe in his dwelling; he will hide me in the shelter of his tabernacle and set me high upon a rock.

Psalm 27:1, 3, 5

It is better to take refuge in the Lord than to trust in man.

Psalm 118:8

Trust in the Lord with all your heart and lean not on your own understanding;

In all your ways acknowledge him, and he will make your paths straight.

Proverbs 3:5, 6

For the Lord will be your confidence and will keep your foot from being snared.

Proverbs 3:26

In his heart a man plans his course, but the Lord determines his steps.

Proverbs 16:9

He gives strength to the weary and increases the power of the weak.

Isaiah 40:29

Because the Sovereign Lord helps me, I will not be disgraced.

Isaiah 50:7

Whoever serves me must follow me; and where I am, my servant also will be. My Father will honor the one who serves me.

John 12:26

Love never fails. But where there are prophecies, they will cease; where there are tongues, they will be stilled; where there is knowledge, it will pass away.

Corinthians 13:8

If any of you lacks wisdom, he should ask God, who gives generously to all without finding fault, and it will be given to him.

James 1:5

When You Want To Be a Leader

As for you, if you walk before me in integrity of heart and uprightness, as David your father did; and do all I command and observe my decrees-and laws,

I will establish your royal throne over Israel forever, as

I promised David your father when I said, "You shall never fail to have a man on the throne of Israel."

1 Kings 9:4, 5

If the Lord delights in a man's way, he makes his steps firm.

Psalm 37:23

For the Lord God is a sun and shield; the Lord bestows favor and honor; no good thing does he withhold from those whose walk is blameless.

Psalm 84:11

Good will come to him who is generous and lends freely, who conducts his affairs with justice.

Psalm 112:5

Better a little with righteousness than much gain with injustice.

In his heart a man plans his course, but the Lord determines his steps.

Proverbs 16:8, 9

The Lord abhors dishonest scales, but accurate weights are his delight.

Proverbs 11:1

Whether you turn to the right or to the left, your ears will hear a voice behind you, saying, "This is the way; walk in it."

Isaiah 30:21

This is what the Lord Almighty says: "Administer true justice; show mercy and compassion to one another.

"Do not oppress the widow or the fatherless, the alien or the poor. In your hearts do not think evil of each other."

Zechariah 7:9, 10

For in the same way you judge others, you will be judged, and with the measure you use, it will be measured to you.

Matthew 7:2

But when he, the Spirit of truth, comes, he will guide you into all truth. He will not speak on his own; he will speak only what he hears, and he will tell you what is yet to come.

John 16:13

Peter and the other apostles replied: "We must obey God rather than men!"

Acts 5:29

Because those who are led by the Spirit of God are sons of God.

Romans 8:14

I urge, then, first of all, that requests, prayers, intercession and thanksgiving be made for everyone —

For kings and all those in authority, that we may live peaceful and quiet lives in all godliness and holiness.

1 Timothy 2:1, 2

Submit yourselves for the Lord's sake to every authority instituted among men: whether to the king, as the supreme authority,

Or to governors, who are sent by him to punish those who do wrong and to commend those who do right.

For it is God's will that by doing good you should silence the ignorant talk of foolish men.

1 Peter 2:13-15

When You Want To Be Faithful

And though she spoke to Joseph day after day, he refused to go to bed with her or even be with her.

One day he went into the house to attend to his duties, and none of the household servants was inside.

She caught him by his cloak and said, "Come to bed with me!"But he left his cloak in her hand and ran out of the house.

Genesis 39:10-12

My times are in your hands; deliver me from my enemies and from those who pursue me.

Let your face shine on your servant; save me in your unfailing love.

Psalm 31:15, 16

You are my hiding place; you will protect me from trouble and surround me with songs of deliverance. Selah

Psalm 32:7

For the Lord will be your confidence.

Proverbs 3:26

But those who hope in the Lord will renew their strength. They will soar on wings like eagles; they will run and not grow weary, they will walk and not be faint.

Isaiah 40:31

So in everything, do to others what you would have them do to you, for this sums up the Law and the Prophets.

Matthew 7:12

Flee from sexual immorality. All other sins a man commits are outside his body, but he who sins sexually sins against his own body.

1 Corinthians 6:18

Instead, be kind to each other, tenderhearted, forgiving one another, just as God through Jesus Christ has forgiven you.

Ephesians 4:32 (NLT)

Husbands, love your wives, just as Christ loved the church and gave himself up for her To make her holy, cleansing her by the washing with water through the word, And to present her to himself as a radiant church, without stain or wrinkle or any other blemish; but holy and blameless.

In this same way, husbands ought to love their wives as their own bodies. He who loves his wife loves himself.

After all, no one ever hated his own body, but he feeds and cares for it, just as Christ does the church — for we are members of his body.

"For this reason a man will leave his father and mother and be united to his wife, and the two will become one flesh."

This is a profound mystery —but I am talking about Christ and the church.

However, each one of you also must love his wife as he loves himself, and the wife must respect her husband.

Ephesians 5:25-33

And the peace of God, which transcends all understanding, will guard your hearts and your minds in Christ Jesus.

Finally, brothers, whatever is true, what ever is noble, whatever is right, whatever is pure, whatever is lovely, whatever is admirable — if anything is excellent or praiseworthy —think about such things.

Philippians 4:7, 8

Do not repay evil with evil or insult with insult, but with blessing, because to this you were called so that you may inherit a blessing.

1 Peter 3:9

When You Want To Be Considerate

Refrain from anger and turn from wrath; do not fret —it leads only to evil.

Psalm 37:8

Good will come to him who is generous and lends freely, who conducts his affairs with justice.

Psalm 112:5

A friend loves at all times, and a brother is born for adversity.

Proverbs 17:17

He who is kind to the poor lends to the Lord, and he will reward him for what he has done.

Proverbs 19:17

A generous man will himself be blessed, for he shares his food with the poor.

Proverbs 22:9

He who gives to the poor will lack nothing, but he who closes his eyes to them receives many curses.

Proverbs 28:27

Do to others whatever you would like them to do to you. This is the essence of all that is taught in the law and the prophets.

Matthew 7:12 (NLT)

Give, and it will be given to you. A good measure, pressed down, shaken together and running over, will be poured into your lap. For with the measure you use, it will be measured to you.

Luke 6:38

On the first day of every week, each one of you should set aside a sum of money in keeping with his income, saving it up, so that when I come no collections will have to be made.

1 Corinthians 16:2

Remember this: Who ever sows sparingly will also reap sparingly, and whoever sows generously will also reap generously.

Each man should give what he has decided in his heart to give, not reluctantly or under compulsion, for God loves a cheerful giver.

And God is able to make all grace abound to you, so that in all things at all times, having all that you need, you will abound in every good work.

2 Corinthians 9:6-8

Command those who are rich in this present world not to be arrogant nor to put their hope in wealth, which is so uncertain, but to put their hope in God, who richly provides us with everything for our enjoyment.

Command them to do good, to be rich in good deeds, and to be generous and willing to share.

In this way they will lay up treasure for themselves as a firm foundation for the coming age, so that they may take hold of the life that is truly life.

1 Timothy 6:17-19

If anyone has material possessions and sees his brother in need but has no pity on him, how can the love of God be in him?

Dear children, let us not love with words or tongue but with actions and in truth.

1 John 3:17, 18

The unfolding of your words gives light; it gives understanding to the simple.

Psalm 119:130

When You Need To Pray

Look to the Lord and his strength; seek his face always.

1 Chronicles 16:11

If my people, who are called by my name, will humble themselves and pray and seek my face and turn from their wicked ways, then will I hear from heaven and will forgive their sin and will heal their land.

2 Chronicles 7:14

By day the Lord directs his love, at night his song is with me—a prayer to the God of my life.

Psalm 42:8

Look to the Lord and his strength; seek his face always.

Psalm 105:4

Seek the Lord while he may be found; call on him while he is near.

Isaiah 55:6

But when you pray, go into your room, close the door and pray to your Father, who is unseen. Then your Father, who sees what is done in secret, will reward you.

And when you pray, do not keep on babbling like pagans, for they think they will be heard because of their many words.

Do not be like them, for your Father knows what you need before' you ask him. This, then, is how you should pray: Our Father in heaven, hallowed be your name.

Matthew 6:6-9

If you believe, you will receive whatever you ask for in prayer.

Matthew 21:22

Watch and pray so that you will not fall into temptation. The spirit is willing, but the body is weak.

Matthew 26:41

Very early in the morning, while it was still dark, Jesus got up, left the house and went off to a solitary place, where he prayed.

Mark 1:35

Therefore I tell you, whatever you ask for in prayer, believe that you have received it, and it will be yours.

Mark 11:24

Be on guard! Be alert! You do not know when that time will come.

Mark 13:33

Then Jesus told his disciples a parable to show them that they should always pray and not give up.

Luke 18:1

Be always on the watch, and pray that you may be able to escape all that is about to happen, and that you may be able to stand before the Son of Man.

Luke 21:36

In the same way, the Spirit helps us in our weakness. We do not know what we ought to pray for, but the Spirit himself intercedes for us with groans that words cannot express.

Romans 8:26

Be joyful in hope, patient in affliction, faithful in prayer.

Romans 12:12

And pray in the Spirit on all occasions with all kinds of prayers and requests. With this in mind, be alert and always keep on praying for all the saints.

Ephesians 6:18

Do not be anxious about anything, but in everything, by prayer and petition, with thanksgiving, present your requests to God.

Philippians 4:6

Devote yourselves to prayer, being watchful and thankful.

Colossians 4:2

Pray continually.

1 Thessalonians 5:17

I want men everywhere to lift up holy hands in prayer, without anger or disputing.

1 Timothy 2:8

Let us then approach the throne of grace with confidence,

so that we may receive mercy and find grace to help us in our time of need.

Hebrews 4:16

For the eyes of the Lord are on the righteous and his ears are attentive to their prayer, but the face of the Lord is against those who do evil.

1 Peter 3:12

But you, dear friends, build yourselves up in your most holy faith and pray in the Holy Spirit.

Jude 20

When You Need Forgiveness

If we confess our sins, he is faithful and just and will forgive us our sins and purify us from all unrighteousness.

1 John 1:9

Have mercy on me, O God, according to your unfailing love; according to your great compassion blot but my transgressions. Wash away all my iniquity and cleanse me from my sin. For I know my transgressions, and my sin is always before me. Against you, you only, have I sinned and done what is evil in your sight, so that you are proved right when you speak and justified when you judge.

Psalm 51:1-4

Cleanse me with hyssop, and I will be clean; wash me, and I will be whiter than snow.

Psalm 51:7

Hide your face from my sins and blot out all my iniquity.

Create in me a pure heart, O God, and renew a steadfast spirit within me.

Do not cast me from your presence or take your Holy Spirit from me.

Psalm 51:9-11

Blessed is he whose transgressions are forgiven, whose sins are covered.

Blessed is the man whose sin the Lord does not count against him and in whose spirit is no deceit.

When I kept silent, my bones wasted away through my groaning all day long.

For day and night your hand was heavy upon me; my strength was sapped as in the heat of summer. Selah

Then I acknowledged my sin to you and did not cover up my iniquity. I said, "I will confess my transgressions to the Lord" — and you forgave the guilt of my sin. Selah

Therefore let everyone who is godly pray to you while you may be found; surely when the mighty waters rise, they will not reach him.

Psalm 32:1-6

He who conceals his sins does not prosper, but whoever confesses and renounces them finds mercy.

Proverbs 28:13

Out of the depths I cry to you, O Lord;

O Lord, hear my voice. Let your ears be attentive to my cry for mercy.

If you, O Lord, kept a record of sins, O Lord, who could stand?

But with you there is forgiveness; therefore you are feared.

Psalm 130:1-4

Praise the Lord, O my soul; all my inmost being, praise his holy name. Praise the Lord, O my soul, and forget not all his benefits — Who forgives all your sins and heals all your diseases.

Psalm 103:1-3

The Lord is compassionate and gracious, slow, to anger, abounding in love.

Psalm 103:8

For as high as the heavens are above the earth, so great is his love for those who fear him;

As far as the east is from the west, so far has he removed

our transgressions from us.

As a father has compassion on his children, so the Lord has compassion on those who fear him.

Psalm 103:11-13

For we do not have a high priest who is unable to sympathize with our weaknesses, but we have one who has been tempted in every way, just as we are —yet was without sin.

Let us then approach the throne of grace with confidence, so that we, may receive mercy and find grace to help us in our time of need.

Hebrews 4:15, 16

This is the covenant I will make with them after that time, says the Lord. I will put my laws in their hearts, and I will write them on their minds.

Then he adds: "Their sins and lawless acts I will remember no more."

And where these have been forgiven, there is no longer any sacrifice for sin.

Therefore, brothers, since we have confidence to enter the Most Holy Place by the blood of Jesus,

By a new and living way opened for us through the curtain, that is, his body,

And since we have a great priest over the house of God,

Let us draw near to God with a sincere heart in full assurance of faith, having our hearts sprinkled to cleanse us from a guilty conscience and having our bodies washed with pure water.

Let us hold unswervingly to the hope we profess, for he who promised is faithful.

Hebrews 10:16-23

My eyes will watch over them for their good, and I will bring them back to this land. I will build them up and not tear them down; I will plant them and not uproot them.

I will give them a heart to know me, that I am the Lord. They will be my people, and I will be their God, for they will return to me with all their heart.

Jeremiah 24:6, 7

For the sake of your name, O Lord, forgive my iniquity, though it is great.

Psalm 25:11

When You Need To Forgive

A man's wisdom gives him patience; it is to his glory to overlook an offense.

Proverbs 19:11

Do not gloat when your enemy falls; when he stumbles,

do not let your heart rejoice.

Do not say, "1'11 do to him as he has done to me; I'll pay that man back for what he did."

Proverbs 24:17, 29

If your enemy is hungry, give him food to eat; if he is thirsty, give him water to drink.

Proverbs 25:21

Blessed are the merciful, for they will be shown mercy.

Matthew 5:7

But I tell you, Do not resist an evil person. If someone strikes you on the right cheek, turn to him the other also.

Matthew 5:39

But I tell you: Love your enemies and pray for those who persecute you.

Matthew 5:44

Forgive us our debts, as we also have forgiven our debtors.

For if you forgive men when they sin against you, your heavenly Father will also forgive you.

But if you do not forgive men their sins, your Father will not forgive your sins.

Matthew 6:12, 14, 15

Then Peter came to Jesus and asked, "Lord, how many times shall I forgive my brother when he sins against me?

Up to seven times?"

Jesus answered, "I tell you, not seven times, but seventy-seven times."

Matthew 18:21, 22

And when you stand praying, if you hold anything against anyone, forgive him, so that your Father in heaven may forgive you your sins.

Mark 11:25

So watch yourselves. "If your brother sins, rebuke him, and if he repents, forgive him.

"If he sins against you seven times in a day, and seven times comes back to you and says, 'I repent,' forgive him."

Luke 17:3, 4

If you forgive anyone his sins, they are forgiven; if you do not forgive them, they are not forgiven.

John 20:23

Bless those who persecute you; bless and do not curse. Do not be overcome by evil, but overcome evil with good.

Romans 12:14, 21

Be kind and compassionate to one another, forgiving each other, just as in Christ God forgave you.

Ephesians 4:32

Bear with each other and forgive whatever grievances

you may have against one another. Forgive as the Lord forgave you.

Colossians 3:13

Do not repay evil with evil or insult with insult, but with blessing, because to this you were called so that you may inherit a blessing.

1 Peter 3:9

When You Need Faith

But what does it say? "The word is near you; it is in your mouth and in your heart," that is, the word of faith we are proclaiming.

Romans 10:8

Consequently, faith comes from hearing the message, and the message is heard through the word of Christ.

Romans 10:17

As for God, his way is perfect; the word of the Lord is flawless. He is a shield for all who take refuge in him.

2 Samuel 22:31

The Lord is a refuge for the oppressed, a stronghold in times of trouble.

Those who know your name will trust in you, for you, Lord, have never forsaken those who seek you.

Psalm 9:9, 10

83

It is better to take refuge in the Lord than to trust in man.

It is better to take refuge in the Lord than to trust in princes.

Psalm 118:8, 9

Those who trust in the Lord are like Mount Zion, which cannot be shaken but endures forever.

Psalm 125:1

My help comes from the Lord, the Maker of heaven and earth.

He will not let your foot slip —he who watches over you will riot slumber;

Indeed, he who watches over Israel will neither slumber nor sleep.

Psalm 121:2-4

But let all who take refuge in you be glad; let them ever sing for joy. Spread your protection over them, that those who love your name may rejoice in you.

Psalm 5:11

May the God of hope fill you with all joy and peace as you trust in him, so that you may overflow with hope by the power of the Holy Spirit.

Romans 15:13

And we also thank God continually because, when you

received the word of God, which you heard from us, you accepted it not as the word of men, but as it actually is, the word of God, which is at work in you who believe.

Thessalonians 2:13

But those sacrifices are an annual reminder of sins.

Hebrews 10:3

But my righteous one will live by faith. And if he shrinks back, I will not be pleased with him.

But we are not of those who shrink back and are destroyed, but of those who believe and are saved.

Hebrews 10:38, 39

For everyone born of God overcomes the world. This is the victory that has overcome the world, even our faith.

1 John 5:4

The Lord himself goes before you and will be with you; he will never leave you nor forsake you. Do not be afraid; do not be discouraged.

Deuteronomy 31:8

Early in the morning they left for the Desert of Tekoa. As they set out, Jehoshaphat stood and said, "Listen to me, Judah and people of Jerusalem! Have faith in the Lord your God and you will be upheld; have faith in his prophets and you will be successful."

2 Chronicles 20:20

"Be strong and courageous. Do not be afraid or discouraged because of the king of Assyria and the vast army with him, for there is a greater power with us than with him.

"With him is only the arm of flesh, but with us is the Lord our God to help us and to fight our battles." And the people gained confidence from what Hezekiah the king of Judah said.

2 Chronicles 32:7, 8

Be not afraid, O land; be glad and rejoice. Surely the Lord has done great things.

Joel 2:21

See, he is puffed up; his desires are not upright —but the righteous will live by his faith.

Habakkuk 2:4

David also said to Solomon his son, "Be strong and courageous, and do the work. Do not be afraid or discouraged, for the Lord God, my God, is with you. He will not fail you or forsake you until all the work for the service of the temple of the Lord is finished.

1 Chronicles 28:20

The Lord is my shepherd, I shall not be in want.

Psalm 23:1

When You Need Comfort

And I will ask the Father, and he will give you another

Counselor to be with you forever —

The Spirit of truth. The world cannot accept him, because it neither sees him nor knows him. But you know him, for he lives with you and will be in you.

I will not leave you as orphans; I will come to you.

John 14:16-18

But the Counselor, the Holy Spirit, whom the Father will send in my name, will teach you all things and will remind you of everything I have said to you.

John 14:26

But I tell you the truth: It is for your good that I am going away. Unless I go away, the Counselor will not come to you; but if I go, I will send him to you.

John 16:7

Praise be to the God and Father of our Lord Jesus Christ, the Father of compassion and the God of all comfort,

Who comforts us in all our troubles, so that we can comfort those in any trouble with the comfort we ourselves have received from God.

For just as the sufferings of Christ flow over into our lives, so also through Christ our comfort overflows.

2 Corinthians 1:3-5

For anyone who speaks in a tongue does not speak to men but to God. Indeed, no one understands him; he utters mysteries with his spirit.

But everyone who prophesies speaks to men for their strengthening, encouragement and comfort.

1 Corinthians 14:2, 3

Therefore encourage one another and build each other up, just as in fact you are doing.

1 Thessalonians 5:11

But you, dear friends, build yourselves up in your most holy faith and pray in the Holy Spirit.

Jude 20

David was greatly distressed because the men were talking of stoning him; each one was bitter in spirit because of his sons and daughters. But David found strength in the Lord his God.

1 Samuel 30:6

The eternal God is your refuge, and underneath are the everlasting arms. He will drive out your enemy before you, saying, "Destroy him!"

Deuteronomy 33:27

Even though I walk through the valley of the shadow of death, I will fear no evil, for you are with me; your rod and your staff, they comfort me.

Psalm 23:4

For in the day of trouble he will keep me safe in his dwelling; he will hide me in the shelter of his tabernacle and set me high upon a rock.

Then my head will be exalted above the enemies who surround me; at his tabernacle will I sacrifice with shouts of joy; I will sing and make music to the Lord.

Psalm 27:5, 6

For his anger lasts only a moment, but his favor lasts a lifetime; weeping may remain for a night, but rejoicing comes in the morning.

Psalm 30:5

I will be glad and rejoice in your love, for you saw my affliction and knew the anguish of my soul.

Psalm 31:7

Cast your cares on the Lord and he will sustain you; he will never let the righteous fall.

Psalm 55:22

Record my lament; list my tears on your scroll —are they not in your record?

Then my enemies will turn back when I call for help. By this I will know that God is for me.

In God, whose word I praise, in the Lord, whose word I praise.

Psalm 56:8-10

My comfort in my suffering is this: Your promise preserves my life.

Psalm 119:50

I remember your ancient laws, O Lord, and I find comfort in them.

Psalm 119:52

Your decrees are the theme of my song wherever I lodge.

Psalm 119:54

When You Need Encouragement

When I called, you answered me; you made me bold and stouthearted.

Psalm 138:3

Though I walk in the midst of trouble, you preserve my life; you stretch out your hand against the anger of my foes, with your right hand you save me.

The Lord will fulfill [his purpose] for me; your love, O Lord, endures forever —do not abandon the works of your hands.

Psalm 138:7, 8

But you, O Lord, have mercy on me; raise me up, that I may repay them;

Psalm 41:10

When you pass through the waters, I will be with you; and when you pass through the rivers, they will not sweep over you. When you walk through the fire, you will not be burned; the flames will not set you ablaze.

Isaiah 43:2

The Lord will surely comfort Zion and will look with compassion on all her ruins; he will make her deserts like Eden, her wastelands like the garden of the Lord. Joy and gladness will be found in her, thanksgiving and the sound of singing.

Isaiah 51:3

I, even I, am he who comforts you. Who are you that you fear mortal men, the sons of men, who are but grass.

Isaiali 51:12

"For I know the plans I have for you," declares the Lord, "plans to prosper you and not to harm you, plans to give you hope and a future."

Jeremiah 29:11

May our Lord Jesus Christ himself and God our Father, who loved us and by his grace gave us eternal encouragement and good hope,

Encourage your hearts and strengthen you in every good deed and word.

2 Thessalonians 2:16, 17

God is not unjust; he will not forget your work and the love you have shown him as you have helped his people and continue to help them.

We want each of you to show this same diligence to the very end, in order to make your hope sure.

We do not want you to become lazy, but to imitate those who through faith and patience inherit what has been promised.

Hebrews 6:10-12

But from everlasting to everlasting the Lord's love is with those who fear him, and his righteousness with their children's children.

Psalm 103:17

Be strong and courageous. Do not be afraid or terrified because of them, for the Lord your God goes with you; he will never leave you nor forsake you.

Deuteronomy 31:6

Yet I still belong to you; you hold my right hand.

Psalm 73:23 (NLT)

Have I not commanded you? Be strong and courageous. Do not be terrified; do not be discouraged, for the Lord your God will be with you wherever you go.

Joshua 1:9

So he said to me, "This is the word of the Lord to Zerubbabel: 'Not by might nor by power, but by my Spirit/ says the Lord Almighty."

Zechariah 4:6

Trust in the Lord and do good; dwell in the land and enjoy safe pasture.

Delight yourself in the Lord and he will give you the desires of your heart.

Commit your way to the Lord^trust in him and he will do this:

He will make your righteousness shine like the dawn, the justice of your cause like the noonday sun.

Psalm 37:3-6

Praise our God, O peoples, let the sound of his praise be heard;

He has preserved our lives and kept our feet from slipping.

Psalm 66:8, 9

But thanks be to God, who always leads us in triumphal procession in Christ and through us spreads everywhere the fragrance of the knowledge of him.

2 Corinthians 2:14

I will praise God's name in song and glorify him with thanksgiving.

Psalm 69:30

The poor will see and be glad — you who seek God, may your hearts live!

Psalm 69:32

Being confident of this, that he who began a good work in you will carry it on to completion until the day of Christ Jesus.

Philippians 1:6

The path of the righteous is like the first gleam of dawn, shining ever brighter till the full light of day.

Proverbs 4:18

When You Need Joy

You have made known to me the path of life; you will fill me with joy in your presence, with eternal pleasures at your right hand.

Psalm 16:11

Splendor and majesty are before him; strength and joy in his dwelling place.

1 Chronicles 16:27

And on that day they offered great sacrifices, rejoicing because God had given them great joy. The women and children also rejoiced. The sound of rejoicing in Jerusalem could be heard far away.

Nehemiah 12:43

You have filled my heart with greater joy than when their grain and new wine abound.

Psalm 4:7

I will be glad and rejoice in you; Twill sing praise to your name, O Most High.

Psalm 9:2

The precepts of the Lord are right, giving joy to the heart. The commands of the Lord are radiant, giving light to the eyes.

Psalm 19:8

The Lord is my strength and my shield; my heart trusts in him, and I am helped. My heart leaps for joy and I will give thanks to him in song.

Psalm 28:7

Then my soul will rejoice in the Lord and delight in his salvation.

Psalm 35:9

Will you not revive us again, that your people may rejoice in you?

Psalm 85:6

Blessed are those who have learned to acclaim you, who walk in the light of your presence, O Lord.

They rejoice in your name all day long; they exult in your righteousness.

Psalm 89:15, 16

Shout for joy to the Lord, all the earth.

Worship the Lord with gladness; come before him with joyful songs.

Psalm 100:1, 2

When the Lord brought back the captives to Zion, we were like men who dreamed.

Our mouths were filled with laughter, our tongues with songs of joy. Then it was said among the nations, "The Lord has done great things for them."

Psalm 126:1, 2

When your words came, I ate them; they were my joy and my heart's delight, for I bear your name, O Lord God Almighty.

Jeremiah 15:16

However, do not rejoice that the spirits submit to you, but rejoice that your names are written in heaven.

Luke 10:20

I have told you this so that my joy may be in you and that your joy may be complete.

John 15:11

You have made known to me the paths of life; you will fill me with joy in your presence.

Acts 2:28

And the disciples were filled with joy and with the Holy Spirit.

Acts 13:52

For the kingdom of God is not a matter of eating and drinking, but of righteousness, peace and joy in the Holy Spirit.

Romans 14:17

For you were once darkness, but now you are light in the Lord. Live as children of light.

Ephesians 5:8

Whatever you have learned or received or heard from me, or seen in me—put it into practice. And the God of peace will be with you.

Philippians 4:9

Though you have not seen him, you love him; and even though you do not see him now, you believe in him and are filled with an inexpressible and glorious joy.

1 Peter 1:8

When You Need Healing

Surely he took up our infirmities and carried our sorrows,

yet we considered him stricken by God, smitten l
afflicted.

But he was pierced for our transgressions, he was crushed
for our iniquities; the punishment that brought us peace was
upon him, and by his wounds we are healed.

Isaiah 53:4, 5

When evening came, many who were demon-possessed
were brought to him, and he drove out the spirits with a word
and healed all the sick.

This was to fulfill what was spoken through the prophet
Isaiah: "He took up our infirmities and carried our diseases."

Matthew 8:16, 17

He himself bore our sins in his body on the tree, so
that we might die to sins and live for righteousness; by his
wounds you have been healed.

1 Peter 2:24

Christ redeemed us from the curse of the law by becoming
a curse for us, for it is written: "Cursed is everyone who is
hung on a tree."

Galatians 3:13

He said, "If you listen carefully to the voice of the Lord
your God and do what is right in his eyes, if you pay attention
to his commands and keep all his decrees, I will not bring on

you any of the diseases I brought on the Egyptians, for I am the Lord, who heals you."

Exodus 15:26

Worship the Lord your God, and his blessing will be on your food and water. I will take away sickness from among you,

And none will miscarry or be barren in your land. I will give you a full life span.

Exodus 23:25, 26

With long life will I satisfy him and show him my salvation.

Psalm 91:16

Praise the Lord, O my soul, and forget not all his benefits

Who forgives all your sins and heals all your diseases;

Psalm 103:2, 3

He sent forth his word and healed them; he rescued them from the grave.

Psalm 107:20

So is my word that goes out from my mouth: It will not return to me empty, but will accomplish what I desire and achieve the purpose for which I sent it.

Isaiah 55:11

Every good and perfect gift is from above, coming down

from the Father of the heavenly lights, who does not change like shifting shadows.

James 1:17

A man with leprosy came and knelt before him and said, "Lord, if you are willing, you can make me clean."

Jesus reached out his hand and touched the man. "I am willing," he said. "Be clean!" Immediately he was cured of his leprosy.

Matthew 8:2, 3

How God anointed Jesus of Nazareth with the Holy Spirit and power, and how he went around doing good and healing all who were under the power of the devil, because God was with him.

Acts 10:38

The thief comes only to steal and kill and destroy; I have come that they may have life, and have it to the full.

John 10:10

Jesus Christ is the same yesterday and today and forever.

Hebrews 13:8

Is any one of you sick? He should call the elders of the church to pray over him and anoint him with oil in the name of the Lord.

And the prayer offered in faith will make the sick person

well; the Lord will raise him up. If he has sinned, he will be forgiven.

James 5:14, 15

Dear friend, I pray that you may enjoy good health and that all may go well with you, even as your soul is getting along well.

3 John 2

You, dear children, are from God and have overcome them, because the one who is in you is greater than the one who is in the world.

1 John 4:4

I tell you the truth, if anyone says to this mountain, "Go, throw yourself into the sea," and does not doubt in his heart but believes that what he says will happen, it will be done for him.

Therefore I tell you, whatever you ask for in prayer, believe that you have received it, and it will be yours.

Mark 11:23, 24

When You Need Love

And hope does not disappoint us, because God has poured out his love into our hearts by the Holy Spirit, whom he has given us.

Romans 5:5

And this is my prayer: that your love may abound more and more in knowledge and depth of insight, So that you may be able to discern what is best and may be pure and blameless until the day of Christ, Filled with the fruit of righteousness that comes through Jesus Christ —to the glory and praise of God.

Philippians 1:9-11

May the Lord make your love increase and overflow for each other and for everyone else, just as ours does for you. May he strengthen your hearts so that you will be blameless and holy in the presence of our God and Father when our Lord Jesus comes with all his holy ones.

1 Thessalonians 3:12, 13

Now about brotherly love we do not need to write to you, for you yourselves have been taught by God to love each other.

And in fact, you do love all the brothers throughout Macedonia. Yet we urge you, brothers, to do so more and,more.

1 Thessalonians 4:9, 10

May the Lord direct your hearts into God's love and Christ's perseverance.

2 Thessalonians 3:5

This is love: not that we loved God, but that he loved us

and sent his Son as an atoning sacrifice for our sins.

Dear friends, since God so loved us, we also ought to love one another.

No one has ever seen God; but if we love one another, God lives in us and his love is made complete in us.

1 John 4:10-12

And so we know and rely on the love God has for us. God is love. Whoever lives in love lives in God, and God in him.

In this way, love is made complete among us so that we will have confidence on the day of judgment, because in this world we are like him.

There is no fear in love. But perfect love drives out fear, because fear has to do with punishment. The one who fears is not made perfect in love.

John 4:16-18

They want to be teachers of the law, but they do not know what they are talking about or what they so confidently affirm.

1 Timothy 1:7

Hatred stirs up dissension, but love covers over all wrongs.

Proverbs 10:12

Place me like a seal over your heart, like a seal on your

arm; for love is as strong as death, its jealousy unyielding as the grave. It burns like blazing fire, like a mighty flame.

Many waters cannot quench love; rivers cannot wash it away. If one were to give all the wealth of his house for love, it would be utterly scorned.

Song of Songs 8:6, 7

He who covers over an offense promotes love, but whoever repeats the matter separates close friends.

Proverbs 17:9

A friend loves at all times, and a brother is born for adversity.

Proverbs 17:17

Honor your father and mother, and love your neighbor as yourself.

Matthew 19:19

Love the Lord your God with all your heart and with all your soul and with all your strength.

Deuteronomy 6:5

Now I had stayed on the mountain forty days and nights, as I did the first time, and the Lord listened to me at this time also. It was not his will to destroy you.

Deuteronomy 10:10

But be very careful to keep the commandment and the law that Moses the servant of the Lord gave you: to love the Lord your God, to walk in all his ways, to obey his commands, to hold fast to him and to serve him with all your heart and all your soul.

Joshua 22:5

I love the Lord, for he heard my voice; he heard my cry for mercy.

Psalm 116:1

Jesus replied, "I will ask you one question. Answer me, and I will tell you by what authority I am doing these things.

"John's baptism —was it from heaven, or from men? Tell me!"

They discussed it among themselves and said, "If we say, 'From heaven,' he will ask, Then why didn't you believe him?'

"But if we say, 'From men'...." (They feared the people, for everyone held that John really was a prophet.)

So they answered Jesus, "We don't know." Jesus said, "Neither will I tell you by what authority I am doing these things."

Mark 11:29-33

A new command I give you: Love one another. As I have loved you, so you must love one another.

By this all men will know that you are my disciples, if you love one another.

John 13:34, 35

Now about food sacrificed to idols: We know that we all possess knowledge. Knowledge puffs up, but love builds up.

1 Corinthians 8:1

The goal of this command is love, which comes from a pure heart and a good conscience and a sincere faith.

1 Timothy 1:5

Above all, love each other deeply, because love covers over a multitude of sins.

1 Peter 4:8

Whoever loves his brother lives in the light, and there is nothing in him to make him stumble.

1 John 2:10

When You Need Patience

Be still before the Lord and wait patiently for him; do not fret when men succeed in their ways, when they carry out their wicked schemes.

Refrain from anger and turn from wrath; do not fret —it leads only to evil.

For evil men will be cut off, but those who hope in the Lord will inherit the land.

Psalm 37:7-9

The end of a matter is better than its beginnings and patience is better than pride.

Do not be quickly provoked in your spirit, for anger resides in the lap of fools.

Ecclesiastes 7:8, 9

By standing firm you will gain life.

Luke 21:19

Not only so, but we also rejoice in our sufferings, because we know that suffering produces perseverance.

Romans 5:3

1\8\16 Let us not become weary in doing good, for at the proper time we will reap a harvest if we do not give up.

Galatians 6:9

As a prisoner for the Lord, then, I urge you to live a life worthy of the calling you have received.

Be completely humble and gentle; be patient, bearing with one another in love.

Ephesians 4:1, 2

And we pray this in order that you may live a life worthy of the Lord and may please him in every way: bearing fruit in every good work, growing in the knowledge of God,

Being strengthened with all power according to his glorious might so that you may have great endurance and patience, and joyfully

Giving thanks to the Father, who has qualified you to share in the inheritance of the saints in the kingdom of light.

Colossians 1:10-12

And we urge you, brothers, warn those who are idle, encourage the timid, help the weak, be patient with everyone.

1 Thessalonians 5:14

May the Lord direct your hearts into God's love and Christ's perseverance.

2 Thessalonians 3:5

But you, man of God, flee from all this, and pursue righteousness, godliness, faith, love, endurance and gentleness.

1 Timothy 6:11

We do not want you to become lazy, but to imitate those who through faith and patience inherit what has been promised.

Hebrews 6:12

And so after waiting patiently, Abraham received what was promised. :

Hebrews 6:15

You need to persevere so that when you have done the will of God, you will receive what he has promised.

Hebrews 10:36

Therefore, since we are surrounded by such a great cloud

of witnesses, let us throw off everything that hinders and the sin that so easily entangles, and let us run with perseverance the race marked out for us.

Hebrews 12:1

Because you know that the testing of your faith develops perseverance.

Perseverance must finish its work so that you may be mature and complete, not lacking anything.

James 1:3, 4

My dear brothers, take note of this: Everyone should be quick to listen, slow to speak and slow to become angry.

James 1:19

Be patient, then, brothers, until the Lord's coming. See how the farmer waits for the land to yield its valuable crop and how patient he is for the autumn and spring rains.

You too, be patient and stand firm, because the Lord's coming is near.

James 5:7, 8

For this very reason, make every effort to add to your faith goodness; and to goodness, knowledge;

And to knowledge, self-control; and to self-control, perseverance; and to perseverance, godliness.

2 Peter 1:5, 6

This calls for patient endurance on the part of the saints

who obey God's commandments and remain faithful to Jesus.

Revelation 14:12

The Lord is not slow in keeping his promise, as some understand slowness. He is patient with you, not wanting anyone to perish, but everyone to come to repentance.

2 Peter 3:9

When You Need Peace

When a man's ways are pleasing to the Lord, he makes even his enemies live at peace with him.

Proverbs 16:7

It is to a man's honor to avoid strife, but every fool is quick to quarrel.

Proverbs 20:3

Also, seek the peace and prosperity of the city to which I have carried you into exile. Pray to the Lord for it, because if it prospers, you too will prosper.

Jeremiah 29:7

Blessed are the peacemakers, for they will be called sons of God.

Matthew 5:9

Submit to God and be at peace with him; in this way prosperity will come to you.

Job 22:21

But if he remains silent, who can condemn him? If he hides his face, who can see him? Yet he is over man and nation alike.

Job 34:29

You will keep in perfect peace him whose mind is steadfast, because he trusts in you.

Trust in the Lord forever, for the Lord, the Lord, is the Rock eternal.

Isaiah 26:3, 4

Lord, you establish peace for us; all that we have accomplished you have done for us.

Isaiah 26:12

Who, then, is the man that fears the Lord? He will instruct him in the way chosen for him.

He will spend his days in prosperity, and his descendants will inherit the land.

Psalm 25:12, 13

Consider the blameless, observe the upright; there is a future for the man of peace.

Psalm 37:37

I will listen to what God the Lord will say; he promises

peace to his people, his saints —but let them not return to folly.

Psalm 85:8

Great peace have they who love your law, and nothing can make them stumble.

Psalm 119:165

Those who trust in the Lord are like Mount Zion, which cannot be shaken but endures forever.

Psalm 125:1

To whom he said, "This is the resting place, let the weary rest"; and, "This is the place of repose" —but they would not listen.

Isaiah 28:12

"The glory of this present house will be greater than the glory of the former house," says the Lord Almighty. "And in this place I will grant peace," declares the Lord Almighty.

Haggai 2:9

My covenant was with him, a covenant of life and peace, and I gave them to him; this called for reverence and he revered me and stood in awe of my name.

Malachi 2:5

To shine on those living in darkness and in the shadow of

death, to guide our feet into the path of peace.

Luke 1:79

Peace I leave with you; my peace I give you. I do not give to you as the world gives.

Do not let your hearts be troubled and do not be afraid.

John 14:27

Therefore, since we have been justified through faith, we have peace with God through our Lord Jesus Christ.

Romans 5:1

For the kingdom of God is not a matter of eating and drinking, but of righteousness, peace and joy in the Holy Spirit.

Romans 14:17

Do not be anxious about anything, but in everything, by prayer and petition, with thanksgiving, present your requests to God.

And the peace of God, which transcends all understanding, will guard your hearts and your minds in Christ Jesus.

Philippians 4:6, 7

Let the peace of Christ rule in your hearts, since as members of one body you were called to peace. And be thankful.

Colossians 3:15

7/15

Now may the Lord of peace himself give you peace at all times and in every way. The Lord be with all of you.   X

2 Thessalonians 3:16

He ransoms me unharmed from the battle waged against me, even though many oppose me.

Psalm 55:18

When You Need Protection

He who dwells in the shelter of the Most High will rest in the shadow of the Almighty.

I will say of the Lord, "He is my refuge and my fortress, my God, in whom I trust."

Surely he will save you from the fowler's snare and from the deadly pestilence.

He will cover you with his feathers, and under his wings you will find refuge; his faithfulness will be your shield and rampart.

You will not fear the terror of night, nor the arrow that flies by day,

Nor the pestilence that stalks in the darkness, nor the plague that destroys at midday.

A thousand may fall at your side, ten thousand at your right hand, but it will not come near you.

You will only observe with your eyes and see the punishment of the wicked.

If you make the Most High your dwelling —even the Lord, who is my refuge —

Then no harm will befall you, no disaster will come near your tent.

For he will command his angels concerning you to guard you in all your ways;

They will lift you up in their hands, so that you will not strike your foot against a stone.

You will tread upon the lion and the cobra; you will trample the great lion and the serpent.

"Because he loves me," says the Lord, "I will rescue him; I will protect him, for he acknowledges my name.

"He will call upon me, and I will answer him; I will be with him in trouble, I will deliver him and honor him.

"With long life will I satisfy him and show him my salvation."

Psalm 91:1-16

Therefore let everyone who is godly pray to you while you may be found; surely when the mighty waters rise, they will not reach him.

You are my hiding place; you will protect me from trouble and surround me with songs of deliverance. Selah

Psalm 32:6, 7

"And I myself will be a wall of fire around it," declares

115

the Lord, "and I will be its glory within."

Zechariah 2:5

God is our refuge and strength, an ever-present help in trouble.

Therefore we will not fear, though the earth give way and the mountains fall into the heart of the sea.

Psalm 46:1,2

As for God, his way is perfect; the word of the Lord is flawless. He is a shield for all who take refuge in him.

2 Samuel 22:31

That is why I am suffering as I am. Yet I am not ashamed, because I know whom I have believed, and am convinced that he is able to guard what I have entrusted to him for that day.

2 Timothy 1:12

To him who is able to keep you from falling and to present you before his glorious presence without fault and with great joy.

Jude 24

When You Need Self-Control

Rather, clothe yourselves with the Lord Jesus Christ, and do not think about how to gratify the desires of the sinful nature.

Romans 13:14

For we know that our old self was crucified with him so that the body of sin might be done away with, that we should no longer be slaves to sin.

Romans 6:6

And put a knife to your throat if you are given to gluttony.

Proverbs 23:2

God is within her, she will not fall; God will help her at break of day.

Psalm 46:5

When I am afraid, I will trust in you.

In God, whose word I praise, in God I trust; I will not be afraid. What can mortal man do to me?

Psalm 56:3, 4

Give us aid against the enemy, for the help of man is worthless.

With God we will gain the victory, and he will trample down our enemies.

Psalm 60:11, 12

Hear my cry, O God; listen to my prayer.

From the ends of the earth I call to you, I call as my heart grows faint; lead me to the rock that is higher than I.

For you have been my refuge, a strong tower against the foe.

I long to dwell in your tent forever and take refuge in the shelter of your wings. Selah

Psalm 61:1-4

He who fears the Lord has a secure fortress, and for his children it will be a refuge.

The fear of the Lord is a fountain of life, turning a man from the snares of death.

Proverbs 14:26, 27

Better a patient man than a warrior, a man who controls his temper than one who takes a city.

Proverbs 16:32

"Everything is permissible for me" — but not everything is beneficial. "Everything is permissible for me" —but I will not be mastered by anything.

1 Corinthians 6:12

I have been crucified with Christ and I no longer live, but Christ lives in me. The life I live in the body, I live by faith in the Son of God, who loved me and gave himself for me.

Galatians 2:20

So I say, live by the Spirit, and you will not gratify the desires of the sinful nature.

Galatians 5:16

Those who belong to Christ Jesus have crucified the sinful nature with its passions and desires.

Galatians 5:24

No one serving as a soldier gets involved in civilian affairs —he wants to please his commanding officer.

2 Timothy 2:4

Dear friends, I urge you, as aliens and strangers in the world, to abstain from sinful desires, which war against your soul.

1 Peter 2:11

Therefore, since Christ suffered in his body, arm yourselves also with the same attitude, because he who has suffered in his body is done with sin.

As a result, he does not live the rest of his earthly life for evil human desires, but rather for the will of God.

1 Peter 4:1, 2

If you find honey, eat just enough —too much of it, and you will vomit.

Proverbs 25:16

Everyone who competes in the games goes into strict training. They do it to get a crown that will not last; but we do it to get a crown that will last forever.

Therefore I do not run like a man running aimlessly; I do not fight like a man beating the air.

No, I beat my body and make it my slave so that after I have preached to others, I myself will not be disqualified for the prize.

1 Corinthians 9:25-27

Let your gentleness be evident to all. The Lord is near.

Philippians 4:5

When You Need Strength

The Lord is my strength and my song; he has become my salvation. He is my God, and I will praise him, my father's God, and I will exalt him.

Exodus 15:2

All his laws are before me; I have not turned away from his decrees.

2 Samuel 22:23

The Lord is my strength and my song; he has become my salvation.

Psalm 118:14

Surely God is my salvation; I will trust and not be afraid. The Lord, the Lord, is my strength and my song; he has become my salvation.

Isaiah 12:2

You armed me with strength for battle; you made my adversaries bow at my feet.

2 Samuel 22:40

It is God who arms me with strength and makes my way perfect.

Psalm 18:32

You armed me with strength for battle; you made my adversaries bow at my feet.

Psalm 18:39

May the words of my mouth and the meditation of my heart be pleasing in your sight, O Lord, my Rock and my Redeemer.

Psalm 19:14

The Lord gives strength to his people; the Lord blesses his people with peace.

Psalm 29:11

Sing for joy to God our strength; shout aloud to the God of Jacob!

Psalm 81:1

My flesh and my heart may fail, but God is the strength of my heart and my portion forever.

Psalm 73:26

A wise man has great power, and a man of knowledge increases strength.

Proverbs 24:5

Trust in the Lord forever, for the Lord, the Lord, is the Rock eternal. Isaiah 26:4

He gives strength to the weary and increases the power of the weak.

Isaiah 40:29

But he said to me, "My grace is sufficient for you, for my power is made perfect in weakness". Therefore I will boast all the more gladly about my weaknesses, so that Christ's power may rest on me.

2 Corinthians 12:9

Summon your power, O God; show us your strength, O God, as you have done before.

Psalm 68:28

Finally, be strong in the Lord and in his mighty power.

Ephesians 6:10

When You Need Wisdom

I keep asking that the God of our Lord Jesus Christ, the glorious Father, may give you the Spirit of wisdom and revelation, so that you may know him better.

I pray also that the eyes of your heart may be enlightened in order that you may know the hope to which he has called you, the riches of his glorious inheritance in the saints, and his incomparably great power for us who believe. That power is like the working of his mighty strength.

Ephesians 1:17-19

For this reason, since the day we heard about you, we have not stopped praying for you and asking God to fill you with the knowledge of his will through all spiritual wisdom and understanding.

Colossians 1:9

If any of you lacks wisdom, he should ask God, who gives generously to all without finding fault, and it will be given to him.

But when he asks, he must believe and not doubt, because he who doubts is like a wave of the sea, blown and tossed by the wind.

That man should not think he will receive anything from the Lord;

He is a doubled-minded man, unstable in all he does.

James 1:5-8

Such "wisdom" does not come down from heaven but is earthly, unspiritual, of the devil.

For where you have envy and selfish ambition, there you

find disorder and every evil practice.

But the wisdom that comes from heaven is first of all pure; then peace-loving, considerate, submissive, full of mercy and good fruit, impartial and sincere.

Peacemakers who sow in peace raise a harvest of righteousness.

James 3:15-18

Whoever loves his brother lives in the light, and there is nothing in him to make him stumble.

But whoever hates his brother is in the darkness and walks around in the darkness; he does not know where he is going, because the darkness has blinded him.

John 2:10, 11

Gall to me and I will answer you and tell you great and unsearchable things you do not know.

Jeremiah 33:3

But you have an anointing from the Holy One, and all of you know the truth.

1 John 2:20

As for you, the anointing you received from him remains in you, and you do not need anyone to teach you. But as his anointing teaches you about all things and as that anointing is real, not counterfeit—just as it has taught you, remain in him.

1 John 2:27

Whether you turn to the right or to the left, your ears will hear a voice behind you, saying, "This is the way; walk in it."

Isaiah 30:21

Do not bring hastily to court, for what will you do in the end if your neighbor puts you to shame?

If you argue your case with a neighbor, do not betray another man's confidence.

Proverbs 25:8, 9

Like an earring of gold or an ornament of fine gold is a wise man's rebuke to a listening ear.

Proverbs 25:12

I will instruct you and teach you in the way you should go; I will counsel you and watch over you.

Psalm 32:8

For with you is the fountain of life; in your light we see light.

Psalm 36:9

The unfolding of your words gives light; it gives understanding to the simple.

Psalm 119:130

If you had responded to my rebuke, I would have poured out my heart to you and made my thoughts known to you.

Proverbs 1:23

For the Lord gives wisdom, and from his mouth come knowledge and understanding.

He holds victory in store for the upright, he is a shield to those whose walk is blameless.

Proverbs 2:6, 7

Send forth your light and your truth, let them guide me; letthem bring me to your holy mountain, to the place where you dwell.

Psalm 43:3

Reflect on what I am saying, for the Lord will give you insight into all this.

2 Timothy 2:7

When You Need Deliverance

My soul finds rest in God alone; my salvation comes from him.

He alone is my rock and my salvation; he is my fortress, I will never be shaken.

Psalm 62:1, 2

Find rest, O my soul, in God alone; my hope comes from him.

He alone is my rock and my salvation; he is my fortress, I will not be shaken.

My salvation and my honor depend on God; he is my

mighty rock, my refuge.

Trust in him at all times, O people; pour out your hearts to him, for God is our refuge. Selah

Psalm 62:5-8

One thing God has spoken, two things have I heard: that you, O God, are strong, and that you, O Lord, are loving. Surely you will reward each person according to what he has done.

Psalm 62:11, 12

If this is so, then the Lord knows how to rescue godly men from trials and to hold the unrighteous for the day of judgment, while continuing their punishment.

2 Peter 2:9

He reached down from on high and took hold of me; he drew me out of deep waters.

He rescued me from my powerful enemy, from my foes, who were too strong for me.

They confronted me in the day of my disaster, but the Lord was my support.

He brought me out into a spacious place; he rescued me because he delighted in me.

Psalm 18:16-19

In the shelter of your presence you hide them from the

intrigues of men; in your dwelling you keep them safe from accusing tongues.

Psalm 31:20

I sought the Lord, and he answered me; he delivered me from all my fears.

Psalm 34:4

A righteous man may have many troubles, but the Lord delivers him from them all.

Psalm 34:19

To the Jews who had believed him, Jesus said, "If you hold to my teaching, you are really my disciples.

"Then you will know the truth, and the truth will set you free."

John 8:31, 32

When Jesus had called the Twelve together, he gave them power and authority to drive out all demons and to cure diseases.

Luke 9:1

He called his twelve disciples to him and gave them authority to drive out evil spirits and to heal every disease and sickness.

Matthew 10:1

I have given you authority to trample on snakes and

scorpions and to overcome all the power of the enemy; nothing will harm you.

Luke 10:19

When evening came, many who were demon-possessed were brought to him, and he drove out the spirits with a word and healed all the sick.

This was to fulfill what was spoken through the prophet Isaiah: "He took up our infirmities and carried our diseases."

Matthew 8:16-17

The Lord will rescue me from every evil attack and will bring me safely to his heavenly kingdom. To him be glory for ever and ever. Amen.

2 Timothy 4:18

When You Need Inner Peace

I will lie down and sleep in peace, for you alone, O Lord, make me dwell in safety.

Psalm 4:8

But the meek will inherit the land and enjoy great peace.

Consider the blameless, observe the upright; there is a future for the man of peace.

Psalm 37:11, 37

I will listen to what God the Lord will say; he promises

peace to his people, his saints — but let them not return to folly.

Psalm 85:8

Great peace have they who love your law, and nothing can make them stumble.

Psalm 119:165

You will keep in perfect peace him whose mind is steadfast, because he trusts in you.

Lord, you establish peace for us; all that we have accomplished you have done for us.

Isaiah 26:3, 12

You will go out in joy and be led forth in peace; the mountains and hills will burst into song before you, and all the trees of the field will clap their hands.

Isaiah 55:12

Those who walk uprightly enter into peace; they find rest as they lie in death.

Isaiah 57:2 Peace

I leave with you; my peace I give you. I do not give to you as the world gives. Do not let your hearts be troubled and do not be afraid.

John 14:27

I have told you these things, so that in me you may have

peace. In this world you will have trouble. But take heart! I have overcome the world.

John 16:33

Therefore, since we have been justified through faith, we have peace with God through our Lord Jesus Christ.

Romans 5:1

The mind of sinful man is death, but the mind controlled by the Spirit is life and peace.

Romans 8:6

Because anyone who serves Christ in this way is pleasing to God and approved by men.

Let us therefore make every effort to do what leads to peace and to mutual edification.

Romans 14:18, 19

May the God of hope fill you with all joy and peace as you trust in him, so that you may overflow with hope by the power of the Holy Spirit.

Romans 15:13

Finally, brothers, good-by. Aim for perfection, listen to my appeal, be of one mind, live in peace. And the God of love and peace will be with you.

2 Corinthians 13:11

Grace and peace to you from God our Father and the Lord Jesus Christ.

Galatians 1:3

But the fruit of the Spirit is love, joy, peace, patience, kindness, goodness, faithfulness, gentleness and self-control.

Galatians 5:22, 23

For he himself is our peace, who has made the two one and has destroyed the barrier, the dividing wall of hostility.

Ephesians 2:14

Do not be anxious about anything, but in everything, by prayer and petition, with thanksgiving, present your requests to God.

And the peace of God, which transcends all understanding, will guard your hearts and your minds in Christ Jesus.

Whatever you have learned or received or heard from me, or seen in me—put it into practice. And the God of peace will be with you.

Philippians 4:6, 7, 9

Let the peace of Christ rule in your hearts, since as members of one body you were called to peace. And be thankful.

Colossians 3:15

When You Need Discernment

But it is the spirit in a man, the breath of the Almighty, that gives him understanding.

Job 32:8

I will praise the Lord, who counsels me; even at night my heart instructs me.

Psalm 16:7

As for God, his way is perfect; the word of the Lord is flawless. He is a shield for all who take refuge in him.

Psalm 18:30

Teach me your way, O Lord; lead me in a straight path because of my oppressors.

Psalm 27:11

Send forth your light and your truth, let them guide me; let them bring me to your holy mountain, to the place where you dwell.

Psalm 43:3

The Lord will fulfill [his purpose] for me; your love, O Lord, endures forever—do not abandon the works of your hands.

Psalm 138:8

Trust in the Lord with all your heart and lean not on your

own understanding; In all your ways acknowledge him, and he will make your paths straight.

Proverbs 3:5, 6

Counsel and sound judgment are mine; I have understanding and power.

Proverbs 8:14

Understanding is a fountain of life to those who have it, but folly brings punishment to fools.

A wise man's heart guides his mouth, and his lips promote instruction.

Proverbs 16:22, 23

By wisdom a house is built, and through understanding it is established;

Through knowledge its rooms are filled with rare and beautiful treasures.

Proverbs 24:3, 4

"For my thoughts are not your thoughts, neither are your ways my ways," declares the Lord.

"As the heavens are higher than the earth, so are my ways higher than your ways and my thoughts than your thoughts."

Isaiah 55:8, 9

Call to me and I will answer you and tell you great and

unsearchable things you do not know.

Jeremiah 33:3

When You Need Ability

I can do everything through him who gives me strength.

Philippians 4:13

You show that you are a letter from Christ, the result of our ministry, written not with ink but with the Spirit of the living God, not on tablets of stone but on tablets of human hearts.

Such confidence as this is ours through Christ before God.

2 Corinthians 3:3, 4

I always thank God for you because of his grace given you in Christ Jesus.

For in him you have been enriched in every way —in all your speaking and in all your knowledge — because our testimony about Christ was confirmed in you.

Therefore you do not lack any spiritual gift as you eagerly wait for our Lord Jesus Christ to be revealed.

1 Corinthians 1:4-7

Each one should use whatever gift he has received to serve others, faithfully administering God's grace in its various forms.

If anyone speaks, he should do it as one speaking the very words of God. If anyone serves, he should do it with the strength God provides, so that in all things God may be praised through Jesus Christ. To him be the glory and the power for ever and ever. Amen.

1 Peter 4:10, 11

And I have filled him with the Spirit of God, with skill, ability and knowledge in all kinds of crafts.

Exodus 31:3

Moreover, I have appointed Oholiab son of Ahisamach, of the tribe of Dan, to help him. Also I have given skill to all the craftsmen to make everything I have commanded you.

Exodus 31:6

Grace and peace be yours in abundance through the knowledge of God and of Jesus our Lord.

His divine power has given us everything we need for life and godliness through our knowledge of him who called us by his own glory and goodness.

2 Peter 1:2, 3

Praise be to the Lord my Rock, who trains my hands for war, my fingers for battle.

Psalm 144:1

Remain in me, and I will remain in you. No branch can bear fruit by itself; it must remain in the vine. Neither can you bear fruit unless you remain in me.

I am the vine; you are the branches. If a man remains in me and I in him, he will bear much fruit; apart from me you can do nothing.

John 15:4, 5

If you remain in me and my words remain in you, ask whatever you wish, and it will be given you.

John 15:7

With your help I can advance against a troop; with my God I can scale a wall.

Psalm 18:29

No, in all these things we are more than conquerors through him who loved us.

Romans 8:37

And my God will meet all your needs according to his glorious riches in Christ Jesus.

Philippians 4:19

When You Need a Friend

You are my hiding place; you will protect me from trouble and surround me with songs of deliverance. Selah

Psalm 32:7

He will call upon me, and I will answer him; I will be with him in trouble, I will deliver him and honor him.

Psalm 91:15

A man of many companions may come to ruin, but there is a friend who sticks closer than a brother.

Proverbs 18:24

A friend loves at all times, and a brother is born for adversity.

Proverbs 17:17

He who walks with the wise grows wise, but a companion of fools suffers harm.

Proverbs 13:20

Do nothing out of selfish ambition or vain conceit, but in humility consider others better than yourselves.

Each of you should look not only to your own interests, but also to the interests of others.

Philippians 2:3, 4

For the Lord God is a sun and shield; the Lord bestows favor and honor; no good thing does he withhold from those whose walk is blameless.

Psalm 84:11

Delight yourself in the Lord and he will give you the desires of your heart.

Psalm 37:4

Where can I go from your Spirit? Where can I flee from your presence?

Psalm 139:7

Even there your hand will guide me, your right hand will hold me fast.

Psalm 139:10

When You Need Motivation

Slaves, obey your earthly masters in everything; and do it, not only when their eye is on you and to win their favor, but with sincerity of heart and reverence for the Lord.

Whatever you do, work at it with all your heart, as working for the Lord, not for men.

Colossians 3:22, 23

Stay in that house, eating and drinking whatever they give you, for the worker deserves his wages. Do not move around from house to house.

Luke 10:7

For this reason I remind you to fan into flame the gift of God, which is in you through the laying on of my hands.

For God did not give us a spirit of timidity, but a spirit of power, of love and of self-discipline.

2 Timothy 1:6, 7

But the men of Israel encouraged one another and again took up their positions where they had stationed themselves the first day.

Judges 20:22

Lazy hands make a man poor, but diligent hands bring wealth.

Proverbs 10:4

Diligent hands will rule, but laziness ends in slave labor.

Proverbs 12:24

Do you see a man skilled in his work? He will serve before kings; he will not serve before obscure men.

Proverbs 22:29

I walk in the way of righteousness, along the paths of justice,

Bestowing wealth on those who love me and making their treasuries full.

Proverbs 8:20, 21

Never be lacking in zeal, but keep your spiritual fervor, serving the Lord.

Romans 12:11

Laziness brings on deep sleep, and the shiftless man goes hungry.

Proverbs 19:15

He who gathers crops in summer is a wise son, but he who sleeps during harvest is a disgraceful son.

Proverbs 10:5

He who works his land will have abundant food, but he

who chases fantasies lacks judgment.

Proverbs 12:11

Dishonest money dwindles away, but he who gathers money little by little makes it grow.

Proverbs 13:11

Do not love sleep or you will grow poor; stay awake and you will have food to spare.

Proverbs 20:13

Make it your ambition to lead a quiet life, to mind your own business and to work with your hands, just as we told you,

So that your daily life may win the respect of outsiders and so that you will not be dependent on anybody.

1 Thessalonians 4:11, 12

For even when we were with you, we gave you this rule: "If a man will not work, he shall not eat."

2 Thessalonians 3:10

When You Need Favor

And the boy Samuel continued to grow in stature and in favor with the Lord and with men.

1 Samuel 2:26

For surely, O Lord, you bless the righteous; you surround them with your favor as with a shield.

Psalm 5:12

For his anger lasts only a moment, but his favor lasts a lifetime; weeping may remain for a night, but rejoicing comes in the morning.

Psalm 30:5

O Lord, when you favored me, you made my mountain stand firm; but when you hid your face, I was dismayed.

Psalm 30:7

I know that you are pleased with me, for my enemy does not triumph over me.

Psalm 41:11

Good will come to him who is generous and lends freely, who conducts his affairs with justice.

Psalm 112:5

I have sought your face with all my heart; be gracious to me according to your promise.

Psalm 119:58

For whoever finds me finds life and receives favor from the Lord.

Proverbs 8:35

A good man obtains favor from the Lord, but the Lord condemns a crafty man.

Proverbs 12:2

Then you will win favor and a good name in the sight of God and man.

Proverbs 3:4

And Jesus grew in wisdom and stature, and in favor with God and men.

Luke 2:52

When You Need To Apologize

Then the Lord your God will restore your fortunes and have compassion on you and gather you again from all the nations where he scattered you.

Deuteronomy 30:3

If my people, who are called by my name, will humble themselves and pray and seek my face and turn from their wicked ways, then will I hear from heaven and will forgive their sin and will heal their land.

2 Chronicles 7:14

Cast your cares on the Lord and he will sustain you; he will never let the righteous fall.

Psalm 55:22

The Lord will fulfill [his purpose] for me; your love, O Lord, endures forever—do not abandon the works of your hands.

Psalm 138:8

So do not fear, for I am with you; do not be dismayed, for I am your God. I will strengthen you and help you; I will uphold you with my righteous right hand.

Isaiah 41:10

I will repay you for the years the locusts have eaten — the great locust and the young locust, the other locusts and the locust swarm — my great army that I sent among you.

Joel 2:25

And we know that in all things God works for the good of those who love him, who have been called according to his purpose.

Romans 8:28

We live by faith, not by sight.

2 Corinthians 5:7

Brothers, if someone is caught in a sin, you who are spiritual should restore him gently. But watch yourself, or you also may be tempted.

Carry each other's burdens, and in this way you will fulfill the law of Christ.

Galatians 6:1, 2

Do nothing out of selfish ambition or vain conceit, but in humility consider others better than yourselves.

Philippians 2:3

Brothers, I do not consider myself yet to have taken hold of it. But one thing I do: Forgetting what is behind and straining toward what is ahead,

I press on toward the goal to win the prize for which God has called me heavenward in Christ Jesus.

Philippians 3:13, 14

Let us hold unswervingly to the hope we profess, for he who promised is faithful.

Hebrews 10:23

And without faith it is impossible to please God, because anyone who comes to him must believe that he exists and that he rewards those who earnestly seek him.

Hebrews 11:6

These have come so that your faith —of greater worth than gold, which perishes even though refined by fire —may be proved genuine and may result in praise, glory and honor when Jesus Christ is revealed.

1 Peter 1:7

But you are a chosen people, a royal priesthood, a holy nation, a people belonging to God, that you may declare the praises of him who called you out of darkness into his wonderful light.

1 Peter 2:9

Cast all your anxiety on him because he cares for you.

1 Peter 5:7

When You Need To Overcome Anger

Do not be quickly provoked in your spirit, for anger resides in the lap of fools.

Ecclesiastes 7:9

The Sovereign Lord has given me an instructed tongue, to know the word that sustains the weary. He wakens me morning by morning, wakens my ear to listen like one being taught.

Isaiah 50:4

Blessed are the peacemakers, for they will be called sons of God.

Matthew 5:9

The mind of sinful man is death, but the mind controlled by the Spirit is life and peace.

Romans 8:6

The acts of the sinful nature are obvious: sexual immorality, impurity and debauchery;

Idolatry and witchcraft; hatred, discord, jealousy, fits of rage, selfish ambition, dissensions, factions

And envy; drunkenness, orgies, and the like. I warn you, as I did before, that those who live like this will not inherit the kingdom of God.

But the fruit of the Spirit is love, joy, peace, patience,

kindness, goodness, faithfulness, gentleness and self-control. Against such things there is no law.

Those who belong to Christ Jesus have crucified the sinful nature with its passions and desires.

Since we live by the Spirit, let us keep in step with the Spirit.

Let us not become conceited, provoking and envying each other.

Galatians 5:19-26

In your anger do not sin: Do not let the sun go down while you are still angry.

Get rid of all bitterness, rage and anger, brawling and slander, along with every form of malice.

Be kind and compassionate to one another, forgiving each other, just as in Christ God forgave you.

Ephesians 4:26, 31, 32

Do nothing out of selfish ambition or vain conceit, but in humility consider others better than yourselves.

Each of you should look not only to your own interests, but also to the interests of others.

Philippians 2:3, 4

My dear brothers, take note of this: Everyone should be quick to listen, slow to speak and slow to become angry,

For man's anger does not bring about the righteous life that God desires.

James 1:19, 20

When You Need To Overcome Resentment

Love is patient, love is kind. It does not envy, it does not boast, it is not proud.

It is not rude, it is not self-seeking, it is not easily angered, it keeps no record of wrongs.

1 Corinthians 13:4, 5

The weapons we fight with are not the weapons of the world. On the contrary, they have divine power to demolish strongholds.

2 Corinthians 10:4

Get rid of all bitterness, rage and anger, brawling and slander, along with every form of malice.

Ephesians 4:31

Finally, be strong in the Lord and in his mighty power.

Ephesians 6:10

Finally, brothers, whatever is true, what ever is noble, whatever is right, whatever is pure, whatever is lovely, whatever is admirable —if anything is excellent or praise worthy —think about such things.

Philippians 4:8

Who is wise and understanding among you? Let him show it by his good life, by deeds done in the humility that comes from wisdom.

For where you have envy and selfish ambition, there you find disorder and every evil practice.

James 3:13, 16

When You Need To Overcome Envy and Jealousy

Keep your tongue from evil and your lips from speaking lies.

Psalm 34:13

Do not fret because of evil men or be envious of those who do wrong.

Psalm 37:1

Do not envy a violent man or choose any of his ways.

Proverbs 3:31

A heart at peace gives life to the body, but envy rots the bones.

Proverbs 14:30

The tongue has the power of life and death, and those who love it will eat its fruit.

Proverbs 18:21

Do not envy wicked men, do not desire their company.

Proverbs 24:1

Place me like a seal over your heart, like a seal on your arm; for love is as strong as death, its jealousy unyielding as the grave. It burns like blazing fire, like a mighty flame.

Song of Songs 8:6

Be perfect, therefore, as your heavenly Father is perfect.

Matthew 5:48

Do not judge, or you too will be judged.

Matthew 7:1

Let us behave decently, as in the daytime, not in orgies and drunkenness, not in sexual immorality and debauchery, not in dissension and jealousy.

Romans 13:13

You are still worldly. For since there is jealousy and quarreling among you, are you not worldly? Are you not acting like mere men?

Corinthians 3:3

Love is patient, love is kind. It does not envy, it does not boast, it is not proud.

Corinthians 13:4

Those who belong to Christ Jesus have crucified the sinful nature with its passions and desires.

Since we live by the Spirit, let us keep in step with the Spirit.

Let us not become conceited, provoking and envying each other.

Galatians 5:24-26

Do not let any unwholesome talk come out of your mouths, but only what is helpful for building others up according to their needs, that it may benefit those who listen.

Get rid of all bitterness, rage and anger, brawling and slander, along with every form of malice.

Ephesians 4:29, 31

When You Need Finances

But remember the Lord your God, for it is he who gives you the ability to produce wealth, and so confirms his covenant, which he swore to your forefathers, as it is today.

Deuteronomy 8:18

For the Lord your God will bless you as he has promised, and you will lend to many nations but will borrow from none. You will rule over many nations but none will rule over you.

Deuteronomy 15:6

The Lord will open the heavens, the storehouse of his bounty, to send rain on your land in season and to bless all the work of your hands. You will lend to many nations but will borrow from none.

Deuteronomy 28:12

If they obey and serve him, they will spend the rest of their days in prosperity and their years in contentment.

Job 36:11

I know that there is nothing better for men than to be happy and do good while they live.

That everyone may eat and drink, and find satisfaction in all his toil —this is the gift of God.

Ecclesiastes 3:12, 13

The thief comes only to steal and kill and destroy; I have come that they may have life, and have it to the full.

John 10:10

Each man should give what he has decided in his heart to give, not reluctantly or under compulsion, for God loves a cheerful giver.

And God is able to make all grace abound to you, so that in all things at all times, having all that you need, you will abound in every good work.

2 Corinthians 9:7, 8

Do not store up for yourselves treasures on earth, where moth and rust destroy, and where thieves break in and steal.

But store up for yourselves treasures in heaven, where moth and rust do not destroy, and where thieves do not break in and steal.

For where your treasure is, there your heart will be also.

Matthew 6:19-21

A faithful man will be richly blessed, but one eager to get rich will not go unpunished.

Proverbs 28:20

Command those who are rich in this present world not to be arrogant nor to put their hope in wealth, which is so uncertain, but to put their hope in God, who richly provides us with everything for our enjoyment.

Command them to do good, to be rich in good deeds, and to be generous and willing to share.

In this way they will lay up treasure for themselves as a firm foundation for the coming age, so that they may take hold of the life that is truly life.

1 Timothy 6:17-19

Will a man rob God? Yet you rob me. But you ask, "How do we rob you?" "In tithes and offerings.

"You are under a curse —the whole nation of you — because you are robbing me.

"Bring the whole tithe into the storehouse, that there may be food in my house. Test me in this," says the Lord Almighty, "and see if I will not throw open the floodgates of heaven and pour out so much blessing that you will not have room enough for it."

Malachi 3:8-10

Not that I am looking for a gift, but I am looking for what may be credited to your account.

I have received full payment and even more; I am amply supplied, now that I have received from Epaphroditus the gifts you sent. They are a fragrant offering, an acceptable sacrifice, pleasing to God.

And my God will meet all your needs according to his glorious riches in Christ Jesus.

Philippians 4:17-19

Give, and it will be given to you. A good measure, pressed down, shaken together and running over, will be poured into your lap. For with the measure you use, it will be measured to you.

Luke 6:38

Remember this: Whoever sows sparingly will also reap sparingly, and whoever sows generously will also reap generously.

2 Corinthians 9:6

One man gives freely, yet gains even more; another withholds unduly, but comes to poverty.

Proverbs 11:24

When You Need Guidance

Because those who are led by the Spirit of God are sons of God.

Romans 8:14

The lamp of the Lord searches the spirit of a man; it searches out his inmost being.

Proverbs 20:27

The watchman opens the gate for him, and the sheep listen to his voice. He calls his own sheep by name and leads them out.

When he has brought out all his own, he goes on ahead of them, and his sheep follow him because they know his voice.

But they will never follow a stranger; in fact, they will run away from him because they do not recognize a stranger's voice.

John 10:3-5

In your unfailing love you will lead the people you have redeemed. In your strength you will guide them to your holy dwelling.

Exodus 15:13

In a desert land he found him, in a barren and howling waste. He shielded him and cared for him; he guarded him as the apple of his eye.

Deuteronomy 32:10

You are my lamp, O Lord; the Lord turns my darkness into light.

2 Samuel 22:29

Because of your great compassion you did not abandon them in the desert. By day the pillar of cloud did not cease to guide them on their path, nor the pillar of fire by night to shine on the way they were to take.

You gave your good Spirit to instruct them. You did not withhold your manna from their mouths, and you gave them water for their thirst.

Nehemiah 9:19, 20

Lead me, O Lord, in your righteousness because of my enemies —make straight your way before me.

Psalm 5:8

He makes me lie down in green pastures, he leads me beside quiet waters,

He restores my soul. He guides me in paths of righteousness for his name's sake.

Psalm 23:2, 3

Guide me in your truth and teach me, for you are God my Savior, and my hope is in you all day long.

Psalm 25:5

He guides the humble in what is right and teaches them his way.

Psalm 25:9

Teach me your way, O Lord; lead me in a straight path because of my oppressors.

Psalm 27:11

Since you are my rock and my fortress, for the sake of your name lead and guide me.

Psalm 31:3

I will instruct you and teach you in the way you should go; I will counsel you and watch over you.

Psalm 32:8

For this God is our God for ever and ever; he will be our guide even to the end.

Psalm 48:14

From the ends of the earth I call to you, I call as my heart grows faint; lead me to the rock that is higher than I.

Psalm 61:2

You guide me with your counsel, and afterward you will take me into glory.

Psalm 73:24

If I rise on the wings of the dawn, if I settle on the far side of the sea,

Even there your hand will guide me, your right hand will hold me fast.

See if there is any offensive way in me, and lead me in the way everlasting.

Psalm 139:24

I will lead the blind by ways they have not known, along unfamiliar paths I will guide them; I will turn the darkness into light before them and make the rough places smooth. These are the things I will do; I will not forsake them.

Isaiah 42:16

This is what the Lord says —your Redeemer, the Holy One of Israel: "I am the Lord your God, who teaches you what is best for you, who directs you in the way you should go."

Isaiah 48:17

The Lord will guide you always; he will satisfy your heeds in a sun-scorched land and will strengthen your frame. You will be like a well-watered garden, like a spring whose waters never fail.

Isaiah 58:11

To shine on those living in darkness and in the shadow of death, to guide our feet into the path of peace.

Luke 1:79

But when he, the Spirit of truth, comes, he will guide you

into all truth. He will not speak on his own; he will speak only what he hears, and he will tell you what is yet to come.

John 16:13

Because you know that the testing of your faith develops perseverance.

James 1:3

Call to me and I will answer you and tell you great and unsearchable things you do not know.

Jeremiah 33:3

Or the word of God is living and active. Sharper than any double-edged sword, it penetrates even to dividing soul and spirit, joints and marrow; it judges the thoughts and attitudes of the heart

Hebrews 4:12

When You Are...

When You Are Anxious

Do not be anxious about anything, but in everything, by prayer and petition, with thanksgiving, present your requests to God.

And the peace of God, which transcends all understanding, will guard your hearts and your minds in Christ Jesus.

Philippians 4:6, 7

Who of you by worrying can add a single hour to his life?

Since you cannot do this very little thing, why do you worry about the rest?

Luke 12:25, 26

Cast all your anxiety on him because he cares for you.

1 Peter 5:7

Come to me, all you who are weary and burdened, and I will give you rest.

Take my yoke upon you and learn from me, for I am gentle and humble in heart, and you will find rest for your souls.

For my yoke is easy and my burden is light.

Matthew 11:28-30

So do not worry, saying, 'What shall we eat?' or 'What shall we drink?' or 'What shall we wear?'

For the pagans run after all these things, and your heavenly Father knows that you need them.

Matthew 6:31, 32

The one who received the seed that fell among the thorns is the man who hears the word, but the worries of this life and the deceitfulness of wealth choke it, making it unfruitful.

Matthew 13:22

And call upon me in the day of trouble; I will deliver you, and you will honor me.

Psalm 50:15

Cast your cares on the Lord and he will sustain you; he will never let the righteous fall.

Psalm 55:22

In the day of my trouble I will call to you, for you will answer me.

Psalm 86:7

For I am the Lord, your God, who takes hold of your right hand and says to you, Do not fear; I will help you.

Isaiah 41:13

Trust in the Lord with all your heart and lean not on your own understanding;

In all your ways acknowledge him, and he will make your paths straight.

Proverbs 3:5, 6

Praise be to the Lord, to God our Savior, who daily bears our burdens.

Selah Psalm 68:19

I have told you these things, so that in me you may have peace. In this world you will have trouble. But take heart! I have overcome the world.

John 16:33

Some trust in chariots and some in horses, but we trust in the name of the Lord our God.

Psalm 20:7

Peace I leave with you; my peace I give you. I do not give to you as the world gives. Do not let your hearts be troubled and do not be afraid.

John 14:27

Be silent before me, you islands! Let the nations renew their strength! Let them come forward and speak; let us meet together at the place of judgment.

Who has stirred up one from the east, calling him in righteousness to his service? He hands nations over to him and subdues kings before him. He turns them to dust with his sword, to windblown chaff with his bow.

He pursues them and moves on unscathed, by a path his feet have not traveled before.

Isaiah 41:1-3

When You Are Angry

In your anger do not sin: Do not let the sun go down while you are still angry,

And do not give the devil a foothold.

Ephesians 4:26, 27

Refrain from anger and turn from wrath; do not fret —it leads only to evil.

Psalm 37:8

Short-tempered people do foolish things, and schemars are hated.

Proverbs 14:17 (NLT)

Better a patient man than a warrior, a man who controls his temper than one who takes a city.

Proverbs 16:32

A man's wisdom gives him patience; it is to his glory to overlook an offense.

Proverbs 19:11

Do not be quickly provoked in your spirit, for anger resides in the lap of fools.

Ecclesiastes 7:9

My dear brothers, take note of this: Everyone should be quick to listen, slow to speak and slow to become angry.

James 1:19

Do not say, "I'll do to him as he has done to me; I'll pay that man back for what he did."

Proverbs 24:29

If your enemy is hungry, give him food to eat; if he is thirsty, give him water to drink.

Proverbs 25:21

Blessed are the merciful, for they will be shown mercy.

Matthew5:7

But I tell you: Love your enemies and pray for those who persecute you.

Matthew 5:44

Forgive us our debts, as we also have forgiven our debtors.

Matthew 6:12

For if you forgive men when they sin against you, your heavenly Father will also forgive you.

But if you do not forgive men their sins, your Father will not forgive your sins.

Matthew 6:14, 15

If he sins against you seven times in a day, and seven times comes back to you and says, "I repent," forgive him.

Luke 17:4

Do not be overcome by evil, but overcome evil with good.

Romans 12:21

Be kind and compassionate to one another, forgiving each other, just as in Christ God forgave you.

Ephesians 4:32

Bear with each other and forgive whatever grievances you may have against one another. Forgive as the Lord forgave you.

Colossians 3:13

Do not repay evil with evil or insult with insult, but with blessing, because to this you were called so that you may inherit a blessing.

1 Peter 3:9

When You Are Confused

Trust in the Lord with all your heart and lean not on your own understanding; In all your ways acknowledge him, and he will make your paths straight. Do not be wise in your own eyes; fear the Lord and shun evil. This will bring health to your body and nourishment to your bones.

Proverbs 3:5-8

Call to me and I will answer you and tell you great and unsearchable things you do not know.

Jeremiah 33:3

My son, if you accept my words and store up my commands within you,

Turning your ear to wisdom and applying your heart to understanding,

And if you call out for insight and cry aloud for understanding,

And if you look for it as for silver and search for it as for hidden treasure,

Then you will understand the fear of the Lord and find the knowledge of God.

For the Lord gives wisdom, and from his mouth come knowledge and understanding.

He holds victory in store for the upright, he is a shield to those whose walk is blameless,

For he guards the course of the just and protects the way of his faithful ones.

Proverbs 2:1-8

Show me your ways, O Lord, teach me your paths;

Guide me in your truth and teach me, for you are God my Savior, and my hope is in you all day long.

Psalm 25:4, 5

If any of you lacks wisdom, he should ask God, who gives generously to all without finding fault, and it will be given to him.

But when he asks, he must believe and not doubt, because he who doubts is like a wave of the sea, blown and tossed by the wind.

That man should not think he will receive anything from the Lord;

He is a double-minded man, unstable in all he does.

James 7:5-5

For this reason, since the day we heard about you, we have not stopped praying for you and asking God to fill you with the knowledge of his will through all spiritual wisdom and understanding.

Colossians 1:9

When Jesus spoke again to the people, he said, "I am the light of the world. Whoever follows me will never walk in darkness, but will have the light of life."

John 8:12

Teach me your way, O Lord, and I will walk in your truth; give me an undivided heart, that I may fear your name.

Psalm 86:11

They will come with weeping; they will pray as I bring them back. I will lead them beside streams of water on a level path where they will not stumble, because I am Israel's father, and Ephraim is my firstborn son.

Jeremiah 31:9

I will instruct you and teach you in the way you should go; I will counsel you and watch over you.

Psalm 32:8

I will praise the Lord, who counsels me; even at night my heart instructs me.

Psalm 16:7

The unfolding of your words gives light; it gives understanding to the simple.

Psalm 119:130

Open my eyes that I may see wonderful things in your law.

Psalm 119:18

For God is not a God of disorder but of peace. As in all the congregations of the saints.

1 Corinthians 14:33

Reflect on what I am saying, for the Lord will give you insight into all this.

2 Timothy 2:7

When You Are Disappointed Trust in him at all times, O people; pour out your hearts to him, for God is our refuge.

Selah Psalm 62:8

And we know that in all things God works for the good

of those who love him, who have been called according to
his purpose.

Romans 8:28

When You Are Disappointed

Being confident of this, that he who began a good work
in you will carry it on to completion until the day of Christ
Jesus.

Philippians 1:6

I pray also that the eyes of your heart may be enlightened
in order that you may know the hope to which he has called
you, the riches of his glorious inheritance in the saints.

Ephesians 1:18

I have set the Lord always before me. Because he is at
my right hand, I will not be shaken.

Therefore my heart is glad and my tongue rejoices; my
body also will rest secure.

Psalm 16:8-9

God will make this happen, for he who calls you is
faithful.

1 Thessalonians 5:24 (NLT)

Blessed is she who has believed that what the Lord has
said to her will be accomplished!

Luke 1:45

I am with you and will watch over you wherever you go, and I will bring you back to this land. I will not leave you until I have done what I have promised you.

Genesis 28:15

We wait in hope for the Lord; he is our help and our shield.

In him our hearts rejoice, for we trust in his holy name.

May your unfailing love rest upon us, O Lord, even as we put our hope in you.

Psalm 33:20-22

Now to him who is able to do immeasurably more than all we ask or imagine, according to his power that is at work within us.

Ephesians 3:20

The Lord is my strength and my shield; my heart trusts in him, and I am helped. My heart leaps for joy and I will give thanks to him in song.

Psalm 28:7

That is why I am suffering as I am. Yet I am not ashamed, because I know whom I have believed, and am convinced that he is able to guard what I have entrusted to him for that day.

2 Timothy 1:12

God is not a man, that he should lie, nor a son of man,

that he should change his mind. Does he speak and then not act? Does he promise and not fulfill?

Numbers 23:19

For the Lord God is a sun and shield; the Lord bestows favor and honor; no good thing does he withhold from those whose walk is blameless.

Psalm 84:11

Delight yourself in the Lord and he will give you the desires of your heart.

Psalm 37:4

When You Are Frustrated

So he said to me, "This is the word of the Lord to Zerubbabel: 'Not by might nor by power, but by my Spirit,' says the Lord Almighty."

Zechariah 4:6

Peace I leave with you; my peace I give you. I do not give to you as the world gives. Do not let your hearts be troubled and do not be afraid.

John 14:27

There remains, then, a Sabbath-rest for the people of God;

For anyone who enters God's rest also rests from his own work, just as God did from his.

Let us, therefore, make every effort to enter that rest, so that no one will fall by following their example of disobedience.

For the word of God is living and active. Sharper than any double-edged sword, it penetrates even to dividing soul and spirit, joints and marrow; it judges the thoughts and attitudes of the heart.

Hebrews 4:9-12

Let us then approach the throne of grace with confidence, so that we may receive mercy and find grace to help us in our time of need.

Hebrews 4:16

Therefore let everyone who is godly pray to you while you may be found; surely when the mighty waters rise, they will not reach him.

You are my hiding place; you will protect me from trouble and surround me with songs of deliverance. Selah

I will instruct you and teach you in the way you should go; I will counsel you and watch over you.

Do not be like the horse or the mule, which have no understanding but must be controlled by bit and bridle or they will not come to you.

Many are the woes of the wicked, but the Lord's unfailing love surrounds the man who trusts in him.

Rejoice in the Lord and be glad, you righteous; sing, all you who are upright in heart!

Psalm 32:6-11

The path of the righteous is like the first gleam of dawn, shining ever brighter till the full light of day.

Proverbs 4:18

Commit to the Lord whatever you do, and your plans will succeed.

Proverbs 16:3

I am still confident of this: I will see the goodness of the Lord in the land of the living.

Wait for the Lord; be strong and take heart and wait for the Lord.

Psalm 27:13, 14

My flesh and my heart may fail, but God is the strength of my heart and my portion forever.

Those who are far from you will perish; you destroy all who are unfaithful to you.

But as for me, it is good to be near God. I have made the Sovereign Lord my refuge; I will tell of all your deeds.

Psalm 73:26-28

You will keep in perfect peace him whose mind is

steadfast, because he trusts in you. Trust in the Lord forever, for the Lord, the Lord, is the Rock eternal.

Isaiah 26:3, 4

Let us therefore make every effort to do what leads to peace and to mutual edification.

Romans 14:19

Let the peace of Christ rule in your hearts, since as members of one body you were called to peace. And be thankful.

Colossians 3:15

To the Jews who had believed him, Jesus said, "If you hold to my teaching, you are really my disciples.

Then you will know the truth, and the truth will set you free."

John 8:31, 32

When You Are Insecure

I can do everything through him who gives me strength.

Philippians 4:13

For the Lord will be your confidence and will keep your foot from being snared.

Proverbs 3:26

He who fears the Lord has a secure fortress, and for his children it will be a refuge.

Proverbs 14:26

This is what the Sovereign Lord, the Holy One of Israel, says: "In repentance and rest is your salvation, in quietness and trust is your strength, but you would have none of it."

Isaiah 30:15

For I am the Lord, your God, who takes hold of your right hand and says to you, Do not fear; I will help you.

Isaiah 41:13

I am glad I can have complete confidence in you.

2 Corinthians 7:16

I am confident in the Lord that you will take no other view. The one who is throwing you into confusion will pay the penalty, whoever he may be.

Galatians 5:10

For it is we who are the circumcision, we who worship by the Spirit of God, who glory in Christ Jesus, and who put no confidence in the flesh —.

Philippians 3:3

This is the confidence we have in approaching God: that if we ask anything according to his will, he hears us.

1 John 5:14

What, then, shall we say in response to this? If God is for us, who can be against us?

Romans 8:31

No, in all these things we are more than conquerors through him who loved us.

Romans 8:37

In the same way, the Spirit helps us in our weakness. We do not know what we ought to pray for, but the Spirit himself intercedes for us with groans that words cannot express.

Romans 8:26

For everyone born of God overcomes the world. This is the victory that has overcome the world, even our faith.

1 John 5:4

God made him who had no sin to be sin for us, so that in him we might become the righteousness of God.

2 Corinthians 5:21

I keep asking that the God of our Lord Jesus Christ, the glorious Father, may give you the Spirit of wisdom and revelation, so that you may know him better.

I pray also that the eyes of your heart may be enlightened in order that you may know the hope to which he has called you, the riches of his glorious inheritance in the saints.

And his incomparably great power for us who believe. That power is like the working of his mighty strength, which he exerted in Christ when he raised him from the dead and seated him at his right hand in the heavenly realms.

Ephesians 1:17-20

The wicked man flees though no one pursues, but the righteous are as bold as a lion.

Proverbs 28:1

Let us then approach the throne of grace with confidence, so that we may receive mercy and find grace to help us in our time of need.

Hebrews 4:16

So we say with confidence, "The Lord is my helper; I will not be afraid. What can man do to me?"

Hebrews 13:6

When You Are Jealous

Do not fret because of evil men or be envious of those who do wrong.

Psalm 37:1

Be still before the Lord and wait patiently for him; do not fret when men succeed in their ways, when they carry out their wicked schemes.

Psalm 37:7

Anger is cruel and fury overwhelming, but who can stand before jealousy?

Proverbs 27:4

And I saw that all labor and all achievement spring from man's envy of his neighbor. This too is meaningless, a chasing after the wind.

Ecclesiastes 4:4

Let us behave decently, as in the daytime, not in orgies and drunkenness, not in sexual immorality and debauchery, not in dissension and jealousy.

Romans 13:13

You are still worldly. For since there is jealousy and quarreling among you, are you not worldly? Are you not acting like mere men?

1 Corinthians 3:3

Love is patient, love is kind. It does not envy, it does not boast, it is not proud.

Corinthians 13:4

The acts of the sinful nature are obvious: sexual immorality, impurity and debauchery;

Idolatry and witchcraft; hatred, discord, jealousy, fits of rage, selfish ambition, dissensions, factions

And envy; drunkenness, orgies, and the like. I warn you,

as I did before, that those who live like this will not inherit the kingdom of God.

Galatians 5:19-21

Let us not become conceited, provoking and envying each other.

Galatians 5:26

But if you harbor bitter envy and selfish ambition in your hearts, do not boast about it or deny the truth.

James 3:14

Don't grumble against each other, brothers, or you will be judged. The Judge is standing at the door!

James 5:9

So get rid of all evil behavior. Be done with all deceit, hypocrisy, jealousy, and all unkind speech.

1 Peter 2:1 (NLT)

For jealousy arouses a husband's fury, and he will show no mercy when he takes revenge.

Proverbs 6:34

When You Are Lonely

The eternal God is your refuge, and underneath are the everlasting arms. He will drive out your enemy before you, saying, "Destroy him!"

Deuteronomy 33:27

Those who know your name will trust in you, for you, Lord, have never forsaken those who seek you.

Psalm 9:10

Even though I walk through the valley of the shadow of death, I will fear no evil, for you are with me; your rod and your staff, they comfort me.

Psalm 23:4

I was young and now I a mold, yet I have never seen the righteous forsaken or their children begging bread.

Psalm 37:25

For the Lord loves the just and will not forsake his faithful ones. They will be protected forever, but the offspring of the wicked will be cut off.

Psalm 37:28

Keep your lives free from the love of money and be content with what you have, because God has said, "Never will I leave you; never will I forsake you." So we say with confidence, "The Lord is my helper; I will not be afraid. What can man do to me?"

Hebrews 13:5, 6

Vindicate me, O God, and plead my cause against an ungodly nation; rescue me from deceitful and wicked men. You are God my stronghold. Why have you rejected me? Why must I go about mourning, oppressed by the enemy?

Psalm 43:1, 2

What, then, shall we say in response to this? If God is for us, who can be against us?

Romans 8:31

Who shall separate us from the love of Christ? Shall trouble or hardship or persecution or famine or nakedness or danger or sword?

Romans 8:35

No, in all these things we are more than conquerors through him who loved us.

For I am convinced that neither death nor life, neither angels nor demons, neither the present nor the future, nor any powers,

Neither height nor depth, nor anything else in all creation, will be able to separate us from the love of God that is in Christ Jesus our Lord.

Romans 8:37-39

When You Are Persecuted

You, however, know all about my teaching, my way of life, my purpose, faith, patience, love, endurance,

Persecutions, sufferings —what kinds of things happened to me in Antioch, Iconium and Lystra, the persecutions I endured. Yet the Lord rescued me from all of them.

In fact, everyone who wants to live a godly life in Christ Jesus will be persecuted,

181

While evil men and impostors will go from bad to worse, deceiving and being deceived.

But as for you, continue in what you have learned and have become convinced of, because you know those from whom you learned it.

2 Timothy 3:10-14

Blessed are those who are persecuted because of righteousness, for theirs is the kingdom of heaven.

Blessed are you when people insult you, persecute you and falsely say all kinds of evil against you because of me.

Rejoice and be glad, because great is your reward in heaven, for in the same way they persecuted the prophets who were before you.

Matthew 5:10-12

A righteous man may have many troubles, but the Lord delivers him from them all.

Psalm 34:19

The apostles left the Sanhedrin, rejoicing because they had been counted worthy of suffering disgrace for the Name.

Acts 5:41

I am not ashamed of the gospel, because it is the power of God for the salvation of everyone who believes: first for the Jew, then for the Gentile.

For in the gospel a righteousness from God is revealed,

a righteousness that is by faith from first to last, just as it is written: "The righteous will live by faith."

Romans 1:16, 17

He chose to be mistreated along with the people of God rather than to enjoy the pleasures of sin for a short time.

Hebrews 11:25

But how is it to your credit if you receive a beating for doing wrong and endure it? But if you suffer for doing good and you endure it, this is commendable before God.

1 Peter 2:20

And the God of all grace, who called you to his eternal glory in Christ, after you have suffered a little while, will himself restore you and make you strong, firm and steadfast.

1 Peter 5:10

And everyone who has left houses or brothers or sisters or father or mother or children or fields for my sake will receive a hundred times as much and will inherit eternal life.

Matthew 19:29

And as for you, brothers, never tire of doing what is right.

2 Thessalonians 3:13

And for this we labor and strive, that we have put our hope in the living God, who is the Savior of all men, and especially of those who believe.

1 Timothy 4:10

183

He who is not with me is against me, and he who does not gather with me, scatters.

When an evil spirit comes out of a man, it goes through arid places seeking rest and does not find it. Then it says, "I will return to the house I left."

When it arrives, it finds the house swept clean and put in order.

Then it goes and takes seven other spirits more wicked than itself, and they go in and live there. And the final condition of that man is worse than the first.

Luke 11:23-26

Do not be surprised, my brothers, if the world hates you.

1 John 3:13

You, dear children, are from God and have overcome them, because the one who is in you is greater than the one who is in the world.

They are from the world and therefore speak from the viewpoint of the world, and the world listens to them.

We are from God, and whoever knows God listens to us; but whoever is not from God does not listen to us. This is how we recognize the Spirit of truth and the spirit of falsehood.

1 John 4:4-6

When You Are Uncertain

I am still confident of this: I will see the goodness of the Lord in the land of the living.

Wait for the Lord; be strong and take heart and wait for the Lord.

Psalm 27:13, 14

Let us hold unswervingly to the hope we profess, for he who promised is faithful.

Hebrews 10:23

But when he asks, he must believe and not doubt, because he who doubts is like a wave of the sea, blown and tossed by the wind.

James 1:6

Also the plants along the Nile, at the mouth of the river. Every sown field along the Nile will become parched, will blow away and be no more.

Isaiah 19:7

Your statutes stand firm; holiness adorns your house for endless days, O Lord.

Psalm 93:5

All he does is just and good, and all his commandments are trustworthy.

Psalm 111:7 (NLT)

Nevertheless, God's solid foundation stands firm, sealed with this inscription: "The Lord knows those who are his," and, "Everyone who confesses the name of the Lord must turn away from wickedness."

2 Timothy 2:19

Teaching you true and reliable words, so that you can give sound answers to him who sent you?

Proverbs 22:21

When You Are Choosing a Career

When You Are Choosing a Career Be strong and courageous. Do not be afraid or terrified because of them, for the Lord your God goes with you; he will never leave you nor forsake you.

Deuteronomy 31:6

You are my lamp, O Lord; the Lord turns my darkness into light.

2 Samuel 22:29

I will instruct you and teach you in the way you should go; I will counsel you and watch over you.

Psalm 32:8

Teach us to number our days aright, that we may gain a heart of wisdom.

Psalm 90:12

Plans fail for lack of counsel, but with many advisers they succeed.

Proverbs 15:22

The purposes of a man's heart are deep waters, but a man of understanding draws them out.

Proverbs 20:5

Apply your heart to instruction and your ears to words of knowledge.

Proverbs 23:12

I will lead the blind by ways they have not known, along unfamiliar paths I will guide them; I will turn the darkness into light before them and make the rough places smooth. These are the things I will do; I will not forsake them.

Isaiah 42:16

Suppose one of you wants to build a tower. Will he not first sit down and estimate the cost to see if he has enough money to complete it?

For if he lays the foundation and is not able to finish it, everyone who sees it will ridicule him,

Saying, "This fellow began to build and was not able to finish."

Luke 14:28-30

Do not let this Book of the Law depart from your mouth; meditate on it day and night, so that you may be careful to do everything written in it. Then you will be prosperous and successful.

Joshua 1:8

When You Are Afraid of the Future

He said: "Listen, King Jehoshaphat and all who live in Judah and Jerusalem! This is what the Lord says to you: 'Do not be afraid or discouraged because of this vast army. For the battle is not yours, but God's.'"

2 Chronicles 20:15

Commit to the Lord whatever you do, and your plans will succeed.

Proverbs 16:3

"Have faith in God," Jesus answered.

"I tell you the truth, if anyone says to this mountain, 'Go, throw yourself into the sea/ and does not doubt in his heart but believes that what he says will happen, it will be done for him."

Mark 11:22, 23

Peace I leave with you; my peace I give you. I do not give to you as the world gives.

Do not let your hearts be troubled and do not be afraid.

John 14:27

Do not be anxious about anything, but in everything, by

prayer and petition, with thanksgiving, present your requests to God.

Philippians 4:6

Let us then approach the throne of grace with confidence, so that we may receive mercy and find grace to help us in our time of need.

Hebrews 4:16

So do not throw away your confidence; it will be richly rewarded.

Hebrews 10:35

Cast all your anxiety on him because he cares for you.

1 Peter5:7

When You Are Looking for a Job

The Lord himself goes before you and will be with you; he will never leave you nor forsake you. Do not be afraid; do not be discouraged.

Deuteronomy 31:8

Fearing people is a dangerous trap, but trusting the Lord means safety.

Proverbs 29:25 (NLT)

Whether you turn to the right or to the left, your ears will hear a voice behind you, saying, "This is the way; walk in it."

Isaiah 30:21

This is what the Lord says —your Redeemer, the Holy One of Israel: "I am the Lord your God, who teaches you what is best for you, who directs you in the way you should go."

Isaiah 48:17

But blessed is the man who trusts in the Lord, whose confidence is in him.

Jeremiah 17:7

Do not be like them, for your Father knows what you need before you ask him.

Matthew 6:8

Look at the birds of the air; they do not sow or reap or store away in barns, and yet your heavenly Father feeds them. Are you not much more valuable than they?

Matthew 6:26

"'If you can'?" said Jesus. "Everything is possible for him who believes."

Mark 9:23

And God is able to make all grace abound to you, so that in all things at all times, having all that you need, you will abound in every good work.

2 Corinthians 9:8

When You Are Facing Marital Problems

The Lord God said, "It is not good for the man to be alone. I will make a helper suitable for him."

For this reason a man will leave his father and mother and be united to his wife, and they will become one flesh.

Genesis 2:18, 24

The Lord is my light and my salvation — whom shall I fear? The Lord is the stronghold of my life — of whom shall I be afraid?

Psalm 27:1

Hatred stirs up dissension, but love covers over all wrongs.

Proverbs 10:12

So do not fear, for I am with you; do not be dismayed, for I am your God. I will strengthen you and help you; I will uphold you with my righteous right hand.

Isaiah 41:10

And provide for those who grieve in Zion — to bestow on them a crown of beauty instead of ashes, the oil of gladness instead of mourning, and a garment of praise instead of a spirit of despair. They will be called oaks of righteousness, a planting of the Lord for the display of his splendor.

They will rebuild the ancient ruins and restore the places

long devastated; they will renew the ruined cities that have been devastated for generations.

Isaiah 61:3, 4

For if you forgive men when they sin against you, your heavenly Father will also forgive you.

But if you do not forgive men their sins, your Father will not forgive your sins.

Matthew 6:14, 15

Some Pharisees came and tested him by asking, "Is it lawful for a man to divorce his wife?"

"What did Moses command you?" he replied.

They said, "Moses permitted a man to write a certificate of divorce and send her away."

"It was because your hearts were hard that Moses wrote you this law," Jesus replied.

"But at the beginning of creation God 'made them male and female.'

Therefore what God has joined together, let man not separate."

Mark 10:2-6, 9

Do not deprive each other except by mutual consent and for a time, so that you may devote yourselves to prayer. Then come together again so that Satan will not tempt you because of your lack of self-control.

To the married I give this command (not I, but the Lord): A wife must not separate from her husband.

1 Corinthians 7:5, 10

Love is patient, love is kind. It does not envy, it does not boast, it is not proud.

It always protects, always trusts, always hopes, always perseveres.

1 Corinthians 13:4, 7

Submit to one another out of reverence for Christ.

Wives, submit to your husbands as to the Lord.

Husbands, love your wives, just as Christ loved the church and gave himself up for her.

In this same way, husbands ought to love their wives as their own bodies. He who loves his wife loves himself.

However, each one of you also must love his wife as he loves himself, and the wife must respect her husband.

Ephesians 5:21, 22, 25, 28, 33

Wives, submit to your husbands, as is fitting in the Lord. Husbands, love your wives and do not be harsh with them.

Colossians 3:18, 19

When You Are Overworked

I will lie down and sleep in peace, for you alone, O Lord, make me dwell in safety.

Psalm 4:8

He makes me lie down in green pastures, he leads me beside quiet waters, He restores my soul. He guides me in paths of righteousness for his name's sake.

Psalm 23:2, 3

My heart says of you, "Seek his face!" Your face, Lord, I will seek.

Psalm 27:8

The Lord gives strength to his people; the Lord blesses his people with peace.

Psalm 29:11

Delight yourself in the Lord and he will give you the desires of your heart. Commit your way to the Lord; trust in him and he will do this:

He will make your righteousness shine like the dawn, the justice of your cause like the noonday sun.

Be still before the Lord and wait patiently for him; do not fret when men succeed in their ways, when they carry out their wicked schemes.

But the meek will inherit the land and enjoy great peace.

Psalm 37:4-7, 11

My flesh and my heart may fail, but God is the strength of my heart and my portion forever.

Psalm 73:26

I listen carefully to what God the Lord is saying for he speaks peace to his faithful people. But let them not return to their foolish ways.

Psalm 85:8 (NLT)

You will keep in perfect peace him whose mind is steadfast, because he trusts in you.

Isaiah 26:3

To whom he said, "This is the resting place, let the weary rest"; and, "This is the place of repose" —but they would not listen.

Isaiah 28:12

This is what the Sovereign Lord, the Holy One of Israel, says: "In repentance and rest is your salvation, in quietness and trust is your strength, but you would have none of it."

Isaiah 30:15

Come to me, all you who are weary and burdened, and I will give you rest.

Take my yoke upon you and learn from me, for I am gentle and humble in heart, and you will find rest for your souls.

Matthew 11:28, 29

Then, because so many people were coming and going that they did not even have a chance to eat, he said to them, "Come with me by yourselves to a quiet place and get some rest."

Mark 6:31

Peace I leave with you; my peace I give you. I do not give to you as the world gives. Do not let your hearts be troubled and do not be afraid.

John 14:27

Don't you know that you yourselves are God's temple and that God's Spirit lives in you? If anyone destroys God's temple, God will destroy him; for God's temple is sacred, and you are that temple.

1 Corinthians 3:16, 17

"Everything is permissible" —but not everything is beneficial. "Everything is permissible" —but not everything is constructive.

Corinthians 10:23

When You Are Under Stress

Each one of you will put to flight a thousand of the enemy, for the Lord your God fights for you, just as he has promised.

Joshua 23:10 (NLT)

He will guard the feet of his saints, but the wicked will be silenced in darkness. It is not by strength that one prevails.

1 Samuel 2:9

This is what the Lord says to you: "Do not be afraid or discouraged because of this vast army. For the battle is not yours, but God's."

2 Chronicles 20:15

But you are a shield around me, O Lord; you bestow glory on me and lift up my head.

Psalm 3:3

In the morning, O Lord, you hear my voice; in the morning I lay my requests before you and wait in expectation.

Psalm 5:3

The Lord is a refuge for the oppressed, a stronghold in times of trouble.

Psalm 9:9

I love you, O Lord, my strength.

The Lord is my rock, my fortress and my deliverer; my God is my rock, in whom I take refuge. He is my shield and the horn of my salvation, my stronghold.

Psalm 18:1, 2

Though an army besiege me, my heart will not fear; though war break out against me, even then will I be confident.

For in the day of trouble he will keep me safe in his dwelling; he will hide me in the shelter of his tabernacle and set me high upon a rock.

Psalm 27:3, 5

My flesh and my heart may fail, but God is the strength of my heart and my portion forever.

Psalm 73:26

Praise the Lord, O my soul, and forget not all his benefits

Who satisfies your desires with good things so that your youth is renewed like the eagle's.

Psalm 103:2, 5

He sent out his word and healed them, snatching them from the door of death.

Psalm 107:20 (NLT)

May there be peace within your walls and security within your citadels.

Psalm 122:7

In vain you rise early and stay up late, toiling for food to eat —for he grants sleep to those he loves.

Psalm 127:2

I will praise you, O Lord, with all my heart; before the "gods" I will sing your praise.

Psalm 138:1

When you lie down, you will not be afraid; when you lie down, your sleep will be sweet.

Proverbs 3:24

Wicked men are overthrown and are no more, but the house of the righteous stands firm.

Proverbs 12:7

He who fears the Lord has a secure fortress, and for his children it will be a refuge.

Proverbs 14:26

He gives strength to the weary and increases the power of the weak.

But those who hope in the Lord will renew their strength. They will soar on wings like eagles; they will run and not grow weary, they will walk and not be faint.

Isaiah 40:29, 31

So do not fear, for I am with you; do not be dismayed, for I am your God. I will strengthen you and help you; I will uphold you with my righteous right hand.

Isaiah 41:10

"Not by might nor by power, but by my Spirit," says the Lord Almighty.

Zechariah 4:66

I tell you the truth, whatever you bind on earth will be

bound in heaven, and whatever you loose on earth will be loosed in heaven.

Matthew 18:18

Do not let your hearts be troubled. Trust in God; trust also in me.

Peace I leave with you; my peace I give you. I do not give to you as the world gives. Do not let your hearts be troubled and do not be afraid.

John 14:1, 27

Do not be anxious about anything, but in everything, by prayer and petition, with thanksgiving, present your requests to God.

And the peace of God, which transcends all understanding, will guard your hearts and your minds in Christ Jesus.

Philippians 4:6, 7

Cast all your anxiety on him because he cares for you.

1 Peter 5:7

If this is so, then the Lord knows how to rescue godly men from trials and to hold the unrighteous for the day of judgment, while continuing their punishment.

2 Peter 2:9

When You Are Offended

Do not seek revenge or bear a grudge against one of your people, but love your neighbor as yourself. I am the Lord.

Leviticus 19:18

O Lord my God, I take refuge in you; save and deliver me from all who pursue me.

Psalm 7:1

Those who know your name will trust in you, for you, Lord, have never forsaken those who seek you.

Psalm 9:10

"Because he loves me," says the Lord, "I will rescue him; I will protect him, for he acknowledges my name. "He will call upon me, and I will answer him; I will be with him in trouble, I will deliver him and honor him."

Psalm 91:14, 15

For the Lord will not reject his people; he will never forsake his inheritance.

Psalm 94:14

A fool shows his annoyance at once, but a prudent man overlooks an insult.

Proverbs 12:16

Do not say, "I'll pay you back for this wrong!" Wait for the Lord, and he will deliver you.

Proverbs 20:22

But I tell you that anyone who is angry with his brother will be subject to judgment.

Again, anyone who says to his brother, "Raca," is answerable to the Sanhedrin. But anyone who says, "You fool!" will be in danger of the fire of hell.

Matthew 5:22

For if you forgive men when they sin against you, your heavenly Father will also forgive you.

Matthew 6:14

If he sins against you seven times in a day, and seven times comes back to you and says, "I repent," forgive him.

Luke 17:4

Do not repay anyone evil for evil. Be careful to do what is right in the eyes of everybody.

Romans 12:17

Love is patient, love is kind. It does not envy, it does not boast, it is not proud.

1 Corinthians 13:4

But now you must rid yourselves of all such things as these: anger, rage, malice, slander, and filthy language from your lips.

Colossians 3:8

And the Lord's servant must not quarrel; instead, he must be kind to everyone, able to teach, not resentful.

2 Timothy 2:24

But the Lord stood at my side and gave me strength, so that through me the message might be fully proclaimed and all the Gentiles might hear it. And I was delivered from the lion's mouth.

The Lord will rescue me from every evil attack and will bring me safely to his heavenly kingdom. To him be glory for ever and ever. Amen.

2 Timothy 4:17, 18

When You Are Unfulfilled

Blessed is he whose help is the God of Jacob, whose hope is in the Lord his God.

Psalm 146:5

Above all else, guard your heart, for it is the wellspring of life.

Proverbs 4:23

Diligent hands will rule, but laziness ends in slave labor.

Proverbs 12:24

Hope deferred makes the heart sick, but a longing fulfilled is a tree of life.

Proverbs 13:12

Do not love sleep or you will grow poor; stay awake and you will have food to spare.

Proverbs 20:13

Do not let your heart envy sinners, but always be zealous for the fear of the Lord.

There is surely a future hope for you, and your hope will not be cut off.

Proverbs 23:17, 18

Whatever your hand finds to do, do it with all your might.

Ecclesiastes 9:10a

As long as it is day, we must do the work of him who sent me. Night is coming, when no one can work.

John 9:4

The grass withers and the flowers fall, but the word of our God stands forever.

Isaiah 40:8

When You Feel...

When You Feel Disorganized

Show me your ways, O Lord, teach me your paths.

Psalm 25:4

I will instruct you and teach you in the way you should go; I will counsel you and watch over you.

Psalm 32:8

Cast your cares on the Lord and he will sustain you; he will never let the righteous fall.

Psalm 55:22

Trust in the Lord with all your heart and lean not on your own understanding;

In all your ways acknowledge him, and he will make your paths straight.

Proverbs 3:5, 6

In his heart a man plans his course, but the Lord determines his steps.

Proverbs 16:9

Whether you turn to the right or to the left, your ears will hear a voice behind you, saying, "This is the way; walk in it."

Isaiah 30:21

He gives strength to the weary and increases the power of the weak.

Isaiah 40:29

When you pass through the waters, I will be with you; and when you pass through the rivers, they will not sweep over you. When you walk through the fire, you will not be burned; the flames will not set you ablaze.

Isaiah 43:2

Because the Sovereign Lord helps me, I will not be disgraced.

Isaiah 50:7

For God is not a God of disorder but of peace. As in all the congregations of the saints.

1 Corinthians 14:33

Do not be anxious about anything, but in everything, by prayer and petition, with thanksgiving, present your requests to God.

And the peace of God, which transcends all understanding, will guard your hearts and your minds in Christ Jesus.

Philippians 4:6, 7

If any of you lacks wisdom, he should ask God, who gives generously to all without finding fault, and it will be given to him.

James 1:5

When You Feel Overwhelmed

The name of the Lord is a strong tower; the righteous run to it and are safe.

Proverbs 18:10

Whatever your hand finds to do, do it with all your might.

Ecclesiastes 9:10

Now all has been heard; here is the conclusion of the matter: Fear God and keep his commandments, for this is the whole [duty] of man.

Ecclesiastes 12:13

Now it is required that those who have been given a trust must prove faithful.

1 Corinthians 4:2

And we, who with unveiled faces all reflect the Lord's glory, are being transformed into his likeness with ever-increasing glory, which comes from the Lord, who is the Spirit.

2 Corinthians 3:18

For though we live in the world, we do not wage war as the world does.

The weapons we fight with are not the weapons of the world. On the contrary, they have divine power to demolish strongholds.

We demolish arguments and every pretension that sets

itself up against the knowledge of God, and we take captive every thought to make it obedient to Christ.

2 Corinthians 10:3-5

Then we will no longer be infants, tossed back and forth by the waves, and blown here and there by every wind of teaching and by the cunning and craftiness of men in their deceitful scheming.

Instead, speaking the truth in love, we will in all things grow up into him who is the Head, that is, Christ.

Ephesians 4:14, 15

Being confident of this, that he who began a good work in you will carry it on to completion until the day of Christ Jesus.

And this is my prayer: That your love may abound more and more in knowledge and depth of insight,

So that you may be able to discern what is best and may be pure and blameless until the day of Christ.

Philippians 1:6, 9, 10

For this reason, since the day we heard about you, we have not stopped praying for you and asking God to fill you with the knowledge of his will through all spiritual wisdom and understanding.

And we pray this in order that you may live a life worthy of the Lord and may please him in every way: bearing fruit in every good work, growing in the knowledge of God,

Being strengthened with all power according to his glorious might so that you may have great endurance and patience, and joyfully

Giving thanks to the Father, who has qualified you to share in the inheritance of the saints in the kingdom of light.

Colossians 1:9-12

Let the word of Christ dwell in you richly as you teach and admonish one another with all wisdom, and as you sing psalms, hymns and spiritual songs with gratitude in your hearts to God.

Colossians 3:16

When You Feel Robbed of Your Private Time

I have set the Lord always before me. Because he is at my right hand, I will not be shaken.

Psalm 16:8

Vindicate me, O Lord, for I have led a blameless life; I have trusted in the Lord without wavering.

For your love is ever before me, and I walk continually in your truth.

Psalm 26:1, 3

If the Lord delights in a man's way, he makes his steps firm.

Psalm 37:23

Your statutes are my delight; they are my counselors.

Psalm 119:24

The wicked man flees though no one pursues, but the righteous are as bold as a lion.

Proverbs 28:1

Therefore, I urge you, brothers, in view of God's mercy, to offer your bodies as living sacrifices, holy and pleasing to God—this is your spiritual act of worship.

Do not conform any longer to the pattern of this world, but be transformed by the renewing of your mind. Then you will be able to test and approve what God's will is —his good, pleasing and perfect will.

Be devoted to one another in brotherly love. Honor one another above yourselves. Never be lacking in zeal, but keep your spiritual fervor, serving the Lord. Be joyful in hope, patient in affliction, faithful in prayer. Share with God's people who are in need. Practice hospitality.

Romans 12:1, 2, 10-13

Be on your guard; stand firm in the faith; be men of courage; be strong.

1 Corinthians 16:13

We demolish arguments and every pretension that sets itself up against the knowledge of God, and we take captive every thought to make it obedient to Christ.

2 Corinthians 10:5

Therefore each of you must put off falsehood and speak truthfully to his neighbor, for we are all members of one body.

Ephesians 4:25

When You Feel Unqualified for Leadership

But as for you, be strong and do not give up, for your work will be rewarded.

2 Chronicles 15:7

Be strong and take heart, all you who hope in the Lord.

Psalm 31:24

Counsel and sound judgment are mine; I have understanding and power.

Proverbs 8:14

Strengthen the feeble hands, steady the knees that give way.

Isaiah 35:3

So do not fear, for I am with you; do not be dismayed, for I am your God. I will strengthen you and help you; I will uphold you with my righteous right hand.

Isaiah 41:10

The Sovereign Lord is my strength; he makes my feet like the feet of a deer, he enables me to go on the heights. For the director of music. On my stringed instruments.

Habakkuk 3:19

But you will receive power when the Holy Spirit comes on you; and you will be my witnesses in Jerusalem, and in all Judea and Samaria, and to the ends of the earth.

Acts 1:8

But God chose the foolish things of the world to shame the wise; God chose the weak things of the world to shame the strong.

1 Corinthians 1:27

To one there is given through the Spirit the message of wisdom, to another the message of knowledge by means of the same Spirit.

1 Corinthians 12:8

And God is able to make all grace abound to you, so that in all things at all times, having all that you need, you will abound in every good work.

2 Corinthians 9:8

But he said to me, "My grace is sufficient for you, for my power is made perfect in weakness." Therefore I will boast all the more gladly about my weaknesses, so that Christ's power may rest on me.

2 Corinthians 12:9

Now to him who is able to do immeasurably more than all we ask or imagine, according to his power that is at work within us.

Ephesians 3:20

When You Feel Resentful

I will praise the Lord, who counsels me; even at night my heart instructs me.

I have set the Lord always before me. Because he is at my right hand, I will not be shaken.

Therefore my heart is glad and my tongue rejoices; my body also will rest secure.

Psalm 16:7-9

Refrain from anger and turn from wrath; do not fret —it leads only to evil.

Psalm 37:8

Surely you desire truth in the inner parts; you teach me wisdom in the inmost place.

Create in me a pure heart, O God, and renew a steadfast spirit within me.

Psalm 51:6, 10

In God, whose word I praise, in God I trust; I will not be afraid. What can mortal man do to me?

Psalm 56:4

Teach me your way, O Lord, and I will walk in your truth; give me an undivided heart, that I may fear your name.

Psalm 86:11

Trust in the Lord with all your heart and lean not on your own understanding; In all your ways acknowledge him, and he will make your paths straight.

For the Lord will be your confidence. Proverbs 3:5,6,26a A quick-tempered man does foolish things, and a crafty man is hated.

Proverbs 14:17

Better a patient man than a warrior, a man who controls his temper than one who takes a city.

Proverbs 16:32

Fear of man will prove to be a snare, but whoever trusts in the Lord is kept safe.

Proverbs 29:25

Do not be quickly provoked in your spirit, for anger resides in the lap of fools.

Ecclesiastes 7:9

Surely God is my salvation; I will trust and not be afraid. The Lord, the Lord, is my strength and my song; he has become my salvation.

Isaiah 12:2

Blessed are the peacemakers, for they will be called sons of God.

Matthew 5:9

Love is patient, love is kind. It does not envy, it does not boast, it is not proud. It is not rude, it is not self-seeking, it is not easily angered, it keeps no record of wrongs.

1 Corinthians 13:4, 5

The weapons we fight with are not the weapons of the world. On the contrary, they have divine power to demolish strongholds.

2 Corinthians 10:4

But the fruit of the Spirit is love, joy, peace, patience, kindness, goodness, faithfulness, Gentleness and self-control. Against such things there is no law.

Galatians 5:22, 23

He who descended is the very one who ascended higher than all the heavens, in order to fill the whole universe.

Ephesians 4:10

Finally, be strong in the Lord and in his mighty power.

Ephesians 6:10

Finally, brothers, whatever is true, what ever is noble, whatever is right, whatever is pure, whatever is lovely, whatever is admirable —if anything is excellent or praise worthy —think about such things.

Philippians 4:8

Dear friends, do not be surprised at the painful trial you are suffering, as though something strange were happening to you.

1 Peter 4:12

When You Feel Like a Failure

I can do everything through him who gives me strength.

Philippians 4:13

No, in all these things we are more than conquerors through him who loved us.

Romans 8:37

For everyone born of God overcomes the world. This is the victory that has overcome the world, even our faith.

1 John 5:4

I will exalt you, O Lord, for you lifted me out of the depths and did not let my enemies gloat over me.

Psalm 30:1

Do not let this Book of the Law depart from your mouth; meditate on it day and night, so that you may be careful to do everything written in it. Then you will be prosperous and successful.

Joshua 1:8

But you are a shield around me, O Lord; you bestow glory on me and lift up my head.

Psalm 3:3

The Lord sustains the humble but casts the wicked to the ground.

Psalm 147:6

You, dear children, are from God and have overcome them, because the one who is in you is greater than the one who is in the world.

1 John 4:4

But thanks be to God, who always leads us in triumphal procession in Christ and through us spreads everywhere the fragrance of the knowledge of him.

2 Corinthians 2:14

I have been crucified with Christ and I no longer live, but Christ lives in me. The life I live in the body, I live by faith in the Son of God, who loved me and gave himself for me.

Galatians 2:20

Therefore, if anyone is in Christ, he is a new creation; the old has gone, the new has come!

2 Corinthians 5:17

But I have prayed for you, Simon, that your faith may not fail. And when you have turned back, strengthen your brothers.

Luke 22:32

Do not cast me away when I am old; do not forsake me when my strength is gone.

Psalm 71:9

My health may fail, and my sprit may grow weak, but God remains the strength of my heart; he is mine forever.

Psalm 73:26 (NLT)

Now if we are children, then we are heirs —heirs of God and co-heirs with Christ, if indeed we share in his sufferings in order that we may also share in his glory.

Romans 8:17

If you belong to Christ, then you are Abraham's seed, and heirs according to the promise.

Galatians 3:29

When You Feel Threatened

Guide me in your truth and teach me, for you are God my Savior, and my hope is in you all day long.

My eyes are ever on the Lord, for only he will release my feet from the snare.

Psalm 25:5, 15

Summon your power, O God; show us your strength, O God, as you have done before.

Psalm 68:28

Direct my footsteps according to your word; let no sin rule over me.

Psalm 119:133

Do not accuse a man for no reason — when he has done you no harm.

Proverbs 3:30

Pride only breeds quarrels, but wisdom is found in those who take advice.

Proverbs 13:10

A hot-tempered man stirs up dissension, but a patient man calms a quarrel.

Proverbs 15:18

A perverse man stirs up dissension, and a gossip separates close friends.

Proverbs 16:28

Drive out the mocker, and out goes strife; quarrels and insults are ended.

Proverbs 22:10

But those who hope in the Lord will renew their strength. They will soar on wings like eagles; they will run and not grow weary, they will walk and not be faint.

Isaiah 40:31

So do not fear, for I am with you; do not be dismayed, for I am your God. I will strengthen you and help you; I will uphold you with my righteous right hand.

All who rage against you will surely be ashamed and disgraced; those who oppose you will be as nothing and perish.

Isaiah 41:10, 11

Blessed are the peacemakers, for they will be called sons of God.

Matthew 5:9

If your brother sins against you, go and show him his fault, just between the two of you. If he listens to you, you have won your brother over.

Matthew 18:15

If it is possible, as far as it depends on you, live at peace with everyone.

Romans 12:18

Let us therefore make every effort to do what leads to peace and to mutual edification.

Romans 14:19

To one there is given through the Spirit the message of wisdom, to another the message of knowledge by means of the same Spirit.

1 Corinthians 12:8

And without faith it is impossible to please God, because anyone who comes to him, must believe that he exists and that he rewards those who earnestly seek him.

Hebrews 11:6

If any of you lacks wisdom, he should ask God, who gives generously to all without finding fault, and it will be given to him.

James 1:5

For where you have envy and selfish ambition, there you find disorder and every evil practice.

But the wisdom that comes from heaven is first of all pure; then peace-loving, considerate, submissive, full of mercy and good fruit, impartial and sincere.

Peacemakers who sow in peace raise a harvest of righteousness.

James 3:16-18

When You Feel Betrayed

Teach me your way, O Lord; lead me in a straight path because of my oppressors.

Psalm 27:11

Wait for the Lord; be strong and take heart and wait for the Lord.

Psalm 27:14

For I hear the slander of many; there is terror on every side; they conspire against me and plot to take my life..

My times are in your hands; deliver me from my enemies and from those who pursue me.

221

Let your face shine on your servant; save me in your unfailing love.

Psalm 31:13, 15, 16

The angel of the Lord encamps around those who fear him, and he delivers them.

Taste and see that the Lord is good; blessed is the man who takes refuge in him.

Psalm 34:7, 8

Ruthless witnesses come forward; they question me on things I know nothing about. They repay me evil for good and leave my soul forlorn.

Yet when they were ill, I put on sackcloth and humbled myself with fasting. When my prayers returned to me unanswered,

I went about mourning as though for my friend or brother. I bowed my head in grief as though weeping for my mother.

But when I stumbled, they gathered in glee; attackers gathered against me when I was unaware. They slandered me without ceasing.

Let not those gloat over me who are my enemies without cause; let not those who hate me without reason maliciously wink the eye.

They do not speak peaceably, but devise false accusations against those who live quietly in the land.

O Lord, you have seen this; be not silent. Do not be far from me, O Lord.

Psalm 35:11, 13-15, 19, 20, 22

Even my close friend, whom I trusted, he who shared my bread, has lifted up his heel against me.

But you, O Lord, have mercy on me; raise me up, that I may repay them. I know that you are pleased with me, for my enemy does not triumph over me.

Psalm 41.-9-11

If an enemy were insulting me, I could endure it; if a foe were raising himself against me, I could hide from him.

But it is you, a man like myself, my companion, my close friend, with whom I once enjoyed sweet fellowship as we walked with the throng at the house of God.

Psalm 55:12-14

He will cover you with his feathers, and under his wings you will find refuge; his faithfulness will be your shield and rampart. You will not fear the terror of night, nor the arrow that flies by day.

Psalm 91:4, 5

I will set before my eyes no vile thing. The deeds of faithless men I hate; they will not cling to me.

No one who practices deceit will dwell in my house; no one who speaks falsely will stand in my presence.

Psalm 101:3, 7

A truthful witness does not deceive, but a false witness pours out lies.

Proverbs 14:5

Because the Sovereign Lord helps me, I will not be disgraced. Therefore have I set my face like flint, and I know I will not be put to shame.

He who vindicates me is near. Who then will bring charges against me? Let us face each other! Who is my accuser? Let him confront me!

It is the Sovereign Lord who helps me.

Who is he that will condemn me? They will all wear out like a garment; the moths will eat them up.

Isaiah 50:7-9

Do not gloat over me, my enemy! Though I have fallen, I will rise. Though I sit in darkness, the Lord will be my light.

Micah 7:8

Then one of the Twelve —the one called Judas Iscariot —went to the chief priests

And asked, "What are you willing to give me if I hand him over to you?" So they counted out for him thirty silver coins.

From then on Judas watched for an opportunity to hand him over.

Then he returned to the disciples and said to them, "Are you still sleeping and resting? Look, the hour is near, and the Son of Man is betrayed into the hands of sinners."

Matthew 26:14-16, 45

Get rid of all bitterness, rage and anger, brawling and slander, along with every form of malice.

Ephesians 4:31

But the Lord stood at my side and gave me strength, so that through me the message might be fully proclaimed and all the Gentiles might hear it. And I was delivered from the lion's mouth.

2 Timothy 4:17.

Keeping a clear conscience, so that those who speak maliciously against your good behavior in Christ may be ashamed of their slander.

1 Peter 3:16

When You Feel Used

Be strong and courageous. Do not be afraid or terrified because of them, for the Lord your God goes with you; he will never leave you nor forsake you.

Deuteronomy 31:6

Those who know your name will trust in you, for you, Lord, have never forsaken those who seek you.

Psalm 9:10

As for God, his way is perfect; the word of the Lord is flawless. He is a shield for all who take refuge in him.

Psalm 18:30

May the Lord answer you when you are in distress; may the name of the God of Jacob protect you.

May he send you help from the sanctuary and grant you support from Zion.

Psalm 20:1, 2

A righteous man may have many troubles, but the Lord delivers him from them all.

Psalm 34:19

Why are you downcast, O my soul? Why so disturbed within me? Put your hope in God, for I will yet praise him, my Savior and my God.

Psalm 43:5

Find rest, O my soul, in God alone; my hope comes from him.

Psalm 62:5

"Because he loves me," says the Lord, "I will rescue him; I will protect him, for he acknowledges my name.

He will call upon me, and I will answer him; I will be with him in trouble, I will deliver him and honor him."

Psalm 91:14, 15

I wait for the Lord, my soul waits, and in his word I put my hope.

Psalm 130:5

The eyes of all look to you, and you give them their food at the proper time. You open your hand and satisfy the desires of every living thing.

Psalm 145:15, 16

Trust in the Lord with all your heart and lean not on your own understanding; In all your ways acknowledge him, and he will make your paths straight.

Proverbs 3:5, 6

Above all else, guard your heart, for it is the wellspring of life.

Proverbs 4:23

So do not fear, for I am with you; do not be dismayed, for I am your God. I will strengthen you and help you; I will uphold you with my righteous right hand. Isaiah 41:10

Can a mother forget the baby at her breast and have no compassion on the child she has borne? Though she may forget, I will not forget you!

See, I have engraved you on the palms of my hands; your

227

walls are ever before me.

Isaiah 49:15, 16

And teaching them to obey everything I have commanded you. And surely I am with you always, to the very end of the age.

Matthew 28:20

I have given you authority to trample on snakes and scorpions and to overcome all the power of the enemy; nothing will harm you.

Luke 10:19

What, then, shall we say in response to this? If God is for us, who can be against us?

Romans 8:31

So we say with confidence, "The Lord is my helper; I will not be afraid. What can man do to me?"

Hebrews 13:6

Cast all your anxiety on him because he cares for you.

1 Peter 5:7

They overcame him by the blood of the Lamb and by the word of their testimony; they did not love their lives so much as to shrink from death.

Revelation 12:11

Be careful that you do not forget the Lord your God, failing to observe his commands, his laws and his decrees that I am giving you this day.

Deuteronomy 8:11

My son, if sinners entice you, do not give in to them.

Proverbs 1:10

Discretion will protect you, and understanding will guard you.

Proverbs 2:11

When You Feel Like Compromising

Do not set foot on the path of the wicked or walk in the way of evil men.

Avoid it, do not travel on it; turn from it and go on your way.

Proverbs 4:14, 15

Stop listening to instruction, my son, and you will stray from the words of knowledge.

Proverbs 19:27

He who walks righteously and speaks what is right, who rejects gain from extortion and keeps his hand from accepting bribes, who stops his ears against plots of murder and shuts his eyes against contemplating evil —

This is the man who will dwell on the heights, whose refuge will be the mountain fortress. His bread will be supplied, and water will not fail him.

Isaiah 33:15, 16

The one who received the seed that fell among the thorns is the man who hears the word, but the worries of this life and the deceitfulness of wealth choke it, making it unfruitful.

Matthew 13:22

If your hand or your foot causes you to sin cut it off and throw it away. It is better for you to enter life maimed or crippled than to have two hands or two feet and be thrown into eternal fire.

Matthew 18:8

Watch and pray so that you will not fall into temptation. The spirit is willing, but the body is weak.

Matthew 26:41

Therefore do not let sin reign in your mortal body so that you obey its evil desires.

For sin shall not be your master, because you are not under law, but under grace.

Romans 6:12, 14

Do not be overcome by evil, but overcome evil with good.

Romans 12:21

When You Feel like Giving Up

Be strong and courageous, because you will lead these people to inherit the land I swore to their forefathers to give them.

Joshua 1:6

But the men of Israel encouraged one another and again took up their positions where they had stationed themselves the first day.

Judges 20:22

David was greatly distressed because the men were talking of stoning him; each one was bitter in spirit because of his sons and daughters. But David found strength in the Lord his God.

1 Samuel 30:6

Wait for the Lord; be strong and take heart and wait for the Lord.

Psalm 27:14

Be strong and take heart, all you who hope in the Lord.

Psalm 31:24

I wait for you, Lord; you will answer, O Lord my God.

Psalm 38:15

But now, Lord, what do I look for? My hope is in you.

Psalm 39:7

Through you we push back our enemies; through your

name we trample our foes.

Psalm 44:5

But as for me, I will always have hope; I will praise you more and more.

Psalm 71:14

Blessed is he whose help is the God of Jacob, whose hope is in the Lord his God.

Psalm 146:5

Know that the Lord is God. It is he who made us, and we are his; we are his people, the sheep of his pasture.

Psalm 100:3

I lift up my eyes to you, to you whose throne is in heaven.

As the eyes of slaves look to the hand of their master, as the eyes of a maid look to the hand of her mistress, so our eyes look to the Lord our God, till he shows us his mercy.

Psalm 123:1, 2

Trust in the Lord with all your heart and lean not on your own understanding.

Proverbs 3:5

"'If you can'?" said Jesus. "Everything is possible for him who believes."

Immediately the boy's father exclaimed, "I do believe; help me overcome my unbelief!"

Mark 9:23, 24

Therefore I tell you, whatever you ask for in prayer, believe that you have received it, and it will be yours.

Mark 11:24

But if we hope for what we do not yet have, we wait for it patiently.

Who shall separate us from the love of Christ? Shall trouble or hardship or persecution or famine or nakedness or danger or sword?

As it is written: "For your sake we face death all day long; we are considered as sheep to be slaughtered."

No, in all these things we are more than conquerors through him who loved us.

For I am convinced that neither death nor life, neither angels nor demons, neither the present nor the future, nor any powers,

Neither height nor depth, nor anything else in all creation, will be able to separate us from the love of God that is in Christ Jesus our Lord.

Romans 8:25, 35, 36-39

I can do everything through him who gives me strength.

Philippians 4:13

Being strengthened with all power according to his glorious might so that you may have great endurance and patience, and joyfully

Giving thanks to the Father, who has qualified you to share in the inheritance of the saints in the kingdom of light.

Colossians 1:11, 12

Now faith is being sure of what we hope for and certain of what we do not see.

Hebrews 11:1

You, dear children, are from God and have overcome them, because the one who is in you is greater than the one who is in the world.

1 John 4:4

I will instruct you and teach you in the way you should go; I will counsel you and watch over you.

Psalm 32:8

For with you is the fountain of life; in your light we see light.

Psalm 36:9

The Lord will fulfill [his purpose] for me; your love, O Lord, endures forever—do not abandon the works of your hands.

Psalm 138:8

Let the wise listen and add to their learning, and let the discerning get guidance.

Proverbs 1:5

Wisdom is supreme; therefore get wisdom. Though it cost all you have, get understanding.

Proverbs 4:7

Esteem her [wisdom], and she will exalt you; embrace her, and she will honor you.

Proverbs 4:8

Bestowing wealth on those who love me and making their treasuries full.

Proverbs 8:21

The plans of the righteous are just, but the advice of the wicked is deceitful.

Proverbs 12:5

When You Feel Incapable of Achieving Your Goals

Know also that wisdom is sweet to your soul; if you find it, there is a future hope for you, and your hope will not be cut off.

Proverbs 24:14

See, the former things have taken place, and new things I declare; before they spring into being I announce them to you.

Isaiah 42:9

Forget the former things; do not dwell on the past.

See, I am doing a new thing! Now it springs up; do you not perceive it? I am making a way in the desert and streams in the wasteland.

Isaiah 43:18, 19

"For I know the plans I have for you," declares the Lord. "plans to prosper you and not to harm you, plans to give you hope and a future."

Jeremiah 29:11

Then the Lord replied: "Write down the revelation and make it plain on tablets so that a herald may run with it.

For the revelation awaits an appointed time; it speaks of the end and will not prove false. Though it linger, wait for it; it will certainly come and will not delay."

Habakkuk 2:2, 3

The Sovereign Lord is my strength; he makes my feet like the feet of a deer, he enables me to go on the heights. For the director of music. On my stringed instruments.

Habakkuk 3:19

Ask and it will be given to you; seek and you will find; knock and the door will be opened to you.

Matthew 7:7

Do not be anxious about anything, but in everything, by prayer and petition, with thanksgiving, present your requests to God.

Philippians 4:6

When You Feel Anxious About Getting Older

Older Moses was a hundred and twenty years old when he died, yet his eyes were not weak nor his strength gone.

Deuteronomy 34:7

Surely goodness and love will follow me all the days of my life, and I will dwell in the house of the Lord forever.

Psalm 23:6

They will still bear fruit in old age, they will stay fresh and green.

Psalm 92:14

For they will prolong your life many years and bring you prosperity.

Proverbs 3:2

He gives strength to the weary and increases the power of the weak.

Even youths grow tired and weary, and young men stumble and fall;

But those who hope in the Lord will renew their strength. They will soar on wings like eagles; they will run and not grow weary, they will walk and not be faint.

Isaiah 40:29-31

Keep your lives free from the love of money and be content with what you have,

Because God has said, "Never will I leave you; never will I forsake you."

Hebrews 13:5

When You Feel Unfulfilled

Be strong and take heart, all you who hope in the Lord.

Psalm 31:24

I will instruct you and teach you in the way you should go; I will counsel you and watch over you.

Psalm 32:8

I wait for you, O Lord; you will answer, O Lord my God.

Psalm 38:15

Why are you downcast, O my soul? Why so disturbed within me? Put your hope in God, for I will yet praise him, my Savior and my God.

Psalm 43:5

But I will keep on hoping for your help; I will praise you more and more.

Psalm 71:14 (NLT)

PRAYER OF SALVATION

God loves you—no matter who you are, no matter what your past. God loves you so much that He gave His one and only begotten Son for you. The Bible tells us that "...whoever believes in Him shall not perish but have eternal life" (John 3:16 NIV). Jesus laid down His life and rose again so that we could spend eternity with Him in heaven and experience His absolute best on earth. If you would like to receive Jesus into your life, say the following prayer out loud and mean it from your heart.

Heavenly Father, I come to You admitting that I am a sinner. Right now, I choose to turn away from sin, and I ask You to cleanse me of all unrighteousness. I believe that Your Son, Jesus, died on the cross to take away my sins. I also believe that He rose again from the dead so that I might be forgiven of my sins and made righteous through faith in Him. I call upon the name of Jesus Christ to be the Savior and Lord of my life. Jesus, I choose to follow You and ask that You fill me with the power of the Holy Spirit. I declare that right now I am a child of God. I am free from sin and full of the right- eousness of God. I am saved in Jesus' name. Amen.

If you prayed this prayer to receive Jesus Christ as your Savior for the first time, please contact us on the Web at **www.harrisonhouse.com** to receive a free book.

Or you may write to us at

Harrison House • P.O. Box 35035 • Tulsa, Oklahoma 74153

The Harrison House Vision

Proclaiming the truth and the power

Of the Gospel of Jesus Christ

With excellence;

Challenging Christians to

Live victoriously,

Grow spiritually,

Know God intimately.